Oryx Sourcebook Series
in Business and Management

Doing Business
in and with
Latin America

Oryx Sourcebook Series in Business and Management

Oryx Sourcebook Series
in Business and Management

Doing Business in and with Latin America
An Information Sourcebook

by E. Willard Miller and Ruby M. Miller
Paul Wasserman, Series Editor

ORYX PRESS
1987

The rare Arabian Oryx is believed to have inspired the myth of the unicorn. This desert antelope became virtually extinct in the early 1960s. At that time several groups of international conservationists arranged to have 9 animals sent to the Phoenix Zoo to be the nucleus of a captive breeding herd. Today the Oryx population is over 400, and herds have been returned to reserves in Israel, Jordan, and Oman.

Copyright © 1987 by
The Oryx Press
2214 N. Central at Encanto
Phoenix, AZ 85004-1483

Published simultaneously in Canada

Printed and Bound in the United States of America

∞ The paper used in this publication meets the minimum requirements of American National Standard for Information Science—Permanence of Paper for Printed Library Materials, ANSI Z39.48, 1984.

Library of Congress Cataloging-in-Publication Data

Miller, E. Willard (Eugene Willard), 1915-
    Doing business in and with Latin America.

    (Oryx sourcebook series in business and management; no. 3)
    Includes index.
    1. Latin America—Commerce—United States—Bibliog-
raphy.   2. United States—Commerce—Latin America—
Bibliography.   3. Latin America—Foreign economic
relations—United States—Bibliography.   4. United
States—Foreign economic relations—Latin America—
Bibliography.   5. Investments, American—Latin America—
Bibliography.   6. Corporations, American—Latin America—
Bibliography.   7. Latin America—Economic conditions—
1945- —Bibliography.   I. Miller, Ruby M.
II. Title.   III. Series.
Z7164.C8M56   1987   016.3326′73228   86-33280
[HF3230.5]
ISBN 0-89774-308-3

6-20-89 sam

Contents

Introduction

The Latin American and the United States economy are increasingly intertwined. In the past, American industry looked to Latin America primarily as a source of raw materials and a market for finished products. With the rapid industrialization of many Latin American countries such as Mexico and Brazil, the economic relationships are rapidly being altered. For modern-day business transactions to be successful between American and Latin American organizations, there is a fundamental need to be informed about current economic conditions. The goal of this volume is to provide up-to-date information to American businesses who are now having economic relations with Latin America or plan to have such operations in the immediate future.

This volume is divided into four parts. The Core Library Collection lists ninety-nine books that have been written on different economic aspects of the Latin American economy. These books provide a perspective on the economy that is evolving in Latin America. The Latin American economy is based on traditions that are strikingly different from those that molded the North American economy. To be successful in Latin America, businesspeople and industrialists must have a deep understanding of these differences. The volumes selected analyze and interpret not only the present day, but provide a background to modern economic conditions.

The second part, Periodical Literature, lists 597 references from journals and other sources. The journal articles are listed first under topical headings and then by geographic area. Most of the references are later than 1980. Earlier references are listed only when they provide significant background information. Information is greatest for the major countries and least for countries where American economic relations are minimal.

The section entitled Reference Works provides basic reference sources important to this subject area. These include not only general bibliographic references, but company publications, statistical handbooks, special periodicals, bank publications, and United States government publications. Appendices are included that provide lists of embassies, and their addresses, agencies, and associations that can be contacted for further information.

This volume will be of particular importance not only to American business and industrial organizations that are doing business with Latin American business organizations, but it also will be of value to economists, political scientists, geographers, and other professionals, as well as students, who wish to be informed about modern-day economic trends of our southern neighbors.

Core Library Collection

In recent years the business and economic ties between the United States and Latin America have been strengthened. There is a growing, but gradual, recognition that mutual relationships must be encouraged and developed. As a response to this need a large number of volumes have been, and are continuing to be, written. Most of the ninety-nine books in this bibliography have been written in recent years. A few older volumes are included that provide a valuable background and understanding to modern developments. A wide variety of viewpoints are presented so that mutual understandings, which have evolved from two very different cultures, can be appreciated. Information is not equally available for all countries of Latin America. More books have been written on Mexico than on any other country. In contrast, little information is available for such small countries as Paraguay or Guyana. The general books on Latin America place emphasis on the larger countries.

UNITED STATES-LATIN AMERICAN RELATIONS

1. Bodenheimer, Susanne, and Danning, Dave. *Yanqui Dollar: The Contribution of U.S. Private Investment to Underdevelopment in Latin America.* New York: North American Congress in Latin America, 1971. 64 p.

2. Bradford, Colin I., Jr. *Forces for Change in Latin America: U.S. Policy Implications.* Washington, DC: Overseas Development Council, 1971. 80 p.

3. *Conference on Some Economic Aspects of Postwar Inter-American Relations—University of Texas, 1946.* Austin, TX: University of Texas Press, 1946. 117 p.

4. Dominguez, Jorge I. *U.S. Interests and Policies in the Caribbean and Central America.* AEI Special Analyses, No. 81–9. Washington, DC: American Enterprise Institute for Public Policy Research, 1982. 55 p.
   The countries of the Caribbean and Central America in the 1980s are, once again, in the forefront of the U.S. foreign policy agenda. This work

sketches some of the consequences of the cycles of neglect followed by periods of frantic activity and suggests specific propositions that would help the U.S. deal with the region. It is stressed that the Caribbean and Central America are not a single unit in making and implementing policies. U.S. policies are likely to be most effective and low cost in the Caribbean, Panama, and Costa Rica than in the other countries of Central America. Of the problems, the need to defend U.S. political and economic hegemony is most important. Six types of hegemonic policies are sketched and past experience discussed briefly.

5. Dominguez, Jorge I., ed. *Economic Issues and Political Conflict: U.S.-Latin American Relations.* London: Butterworth, 1982. 246 p.
   This book emphasizes the implications of Mexico's internal affairs in relation to its international commitments. More important, there is a focus on the larger concerns of Mexican international relations that include, but are not limited to, Mexican relations with the United States. Because the book is a study of internal Mexican affairs, the author treats the impressive changes that have occurred within Mexico in recent decades that have implications for international relations. Major emphasis is placed on the petroleum industry, agriculture, the automobile industry, and last the international reverberations of a dynamic political economy.

6. Dominguez, Virginia R., and Dominguez, Jorge I. *The Caribbean, Its Implications for the United States.* Headline Series No. 253. New York: Foreign Policy Association, 1981. 80 p.
   Many recent events, such as the exodus of 125,000 Cubans to Florida, the plight of the Haitian "boat people," and the military coups in Grenada, have focused the attention of the United States on the Caribbean. Traditionally, U.S. policy in the Caribbean, when it is said to exist at all, has concentrated on short-term remedies designed to relax political tensions or to ward off perceived political or military threats. Since the Monroe Doctrine in 1823, the U.S. policy has centered primarily on keeping the Caribbean from "falling into the hands" of a rival power. This volume stresses the defects of this policy and consequently the substantial dangers to U.S. interests. The argument is presented that it is in the best interests of the United States to help Caribbean countries cope more effectively with their economic and political problems.

7. Erb, Richard D., and Ross, Stanley R., eds. *United States Relations with Mexico, Context and Content.* American Enterprise Institute for Public Policy Research/Miscellaneous Publications. Washington, DC: American Enterprise Institute for Public Policy Research, 1981. 291 p.
   There is frequently a lack of understanding of the problems that exist between Mexico and the United States. Governmental attention and public awareness most often represent concern aroused by some issue of confrontation or some crisis. As a result, relations too often are conducted in a bristling atmosphere of resentment and distrust. It is the purpose of this volume to look first at some of the conditioning elements that contribute to the context within which U.S.-Mexican relations are conducted. The second and largest section of the book is devoted to an

examination of particular issues that constitute the substance of the bilateral relationship. The third section considers Mexican development stressing economic development policy in Mexico, Mexican industrialization, and integral development.

8. Erb, Richard D., and Ross, Stanley R., eds. *U.S. Policies toward Mexico: Perceptions and Perspectives.* Washington, DC: American Enterprise Institute for Public Policy Research, 1979. 56 p.

9. Fagen, Richard R., ed. *Capitalism and the State in U.S.-Latin American Relations.* Stanford, CA: Stanford University Press, 1979. 446 p.
   This volume presents a wide range of topics on economic and political implications of the relations between the United States and Latin America. Such disparate topics are covered as state monopoly capitalism, international competitiveness of the U.S. economy with particular reference to steel and electronics, stabilization programs of the International Monetary Fund, Peru and the U.S. banks, multinational corporations, U.S.-Brazilian relations, business organizations, and international influence in Mexico. The two basic issues investigated are the nature of contemporary capitalism and the nature of the contemporary state. Closely associated to these fundamental issues are North American exceptionalism in a changing world of institutions, alliances, ideology, values, choices, and policy.

10. Fagen, Richard R., and Pellicer, Olga. eds. *The Future of Central America: Policy Choices for the U.S. and Mexico.* Stanford CA: Stanford University Press, 1983. 228 p.
    The essays of this volume were prepared for the project on United States-Mexico Relations and presented at the conference in Guanajuato, Mexico in June 1982. The chapters focus on the profound crisis that is wracking Central America today. Major sections are devoted to the dimensions of economic policy, economic factors in the evolution, U.S. policy options, and Mexico in Central America. A basic objective of the essays is to analyze the nature of the Central American crisis and the limitations on restructuring domestic policies.

11. Grayson, G. W. *The United States and Mexico: Patterns of Influence.* Praeger Special Studies. New York: Praeger, 1984. 214 p.
    The relations between the United States and Mexico are changing. This volume stresses that, in the interest of friendship and a constructive approach to difficult problems, the relationships must be very different from that of the past when the United States was often a covetous neighbor, rather than a good one. The realization in both countries of a need for basic changes in attitude and approach is a welcome first step. This book assesses these changes. Its special value derives from the analysis of the key issues in the Mexican-U.S. relationship: trade and investment, oil and natural gas, immigration, and Central America.

12. Grunwald, Joseph; Wionczek, Miguel S.; and Carnoy, Martin. *Latin American Economic Integration and U.S. Policy.* Washington, DC: Brookings Institution, 1972. 216 p.
    Latin America's income levels have always been close to the top of the developing world. Therefore relations with both the developed countries

and the Third World have tended to be of a special nature. The essays in this volume deal with the changing character of these relationships. The contributions are grouped into five parts. Part one looks at the region from the outside. Part two analyzes how national economic development and policies affect the external sectors in the region's two largest economies, Brazil and Mexico. Part three deals with the relationships among Latin American countries and other developing countries. The focus of part four is on recent history of the region's economic development, and external financing of development, and part five considers relations with foreign multinational corporations.

13. Hayes, Margaret Daly. *Latin America and the U.S. National Interest: A Basis for U.S. Foreign Policy.* Boulder, CO: Westview Press, 1984. 295 p.
   The author addresses the question, Does the United States have compelling national interest in maintaining close relationships with Latin American countries? The conclusion is yes but for reasons different from those offered in traditional literature or developed by many political or economic analysts. The author's viewpoint is that U.S. interests in Latin America are primarily political and secondarily economic, though economic ties are the basis of the relationship. The argument is made that economic aid to the less developed countries of Latin America will enhance political and economic security to a greater degree than will promoting military alliances that Latin Americans may not really want.

14. Latin American Economic System. *Latin American-U.S. Economic Relations, 1982–1983.* Translation of "Relaciones Económicas de América Latina con Estados Unidos, 1982–1983." Boulder, CO: Westview Press, 1984. 119 p.

15. McBride, Robert H., ed. *Mexico and the United States.* American Assembly. Englewood Cliffs, NJ: Prentice-Hall, 1981. 197 p.

16. Martz, John D., and Schoultz, Lars. *Latin America, the United States, and the Inter-American System.* Westview Special Studies on Latin America and the Caribbean. Boulder, CO: Westview Press, 1980. 272 p.

17. Musgrave, Peggy B., ed. *Mexico and the United States, Studies, in Economic Interaction.* Westview Special Studies in International Economics. Boulder, CO: Westview Press, 1985. 261 p.
   This volume develops the theme that the future of the Mexican economy is highly dependent on the health and vitality of the United States. There is also a recognition that this dependence is mutual. The important problems that are addressed include the key areas of finance, trade and industry, economic fluctuations and growth, and labor markets. In each of these areas the papers highlight elements of economic interdependence and examine mutual approaches to the solutions of the joint problems.

18. Poulson, Barry W., and Osborn, T. Noel, eds. *U.S.-Mexico Economic Relations.* Westview Special Studies in International Economics and Business. Boulder, CO: Westview Press, 1979. 442 p.
   The United States historically has had a profound impact upon the Mexican economy. As a consequence, Mexican economists tend to see

this dependent relationship as the basic source of Mexico's economic problems. In contrast, U.S. economists generally focus on the failures of economic policies pursued by the Mexican government and the implications of economic instability in Mexico. The ideas presented in this volume illustrate the contrasts between these two perspectives. At the same time there are insights into the common ground of mutual understanding necessary to resolve the economic problems between the two countries.

19. Purnell, Susanna W., and Wainstein, Eleanor S. *The Problems of U.S. Businesses Operating Abroad in Terrorist Environments.* Santa Monica, CA: Rand Corporation, 1981. 103 p.

20. Shafer, Robert Jones, and Mabry, Donald. *Neighbors—Mexico and the United States: Wetbacks and Oil.* Chicago: Nelson-Hall, 1981. 241 p.
Mexico stands out from most of the Third World nations because of its size, population, social-political stability, and rapid economic growth. It stands out also because of recent oil discoveries. It now has one of the largest reserves in the world and will be a major oil exporter far into the future. The United States hopes to benefit from the petroleum surplus of its neighbor, but a host of historic and current problems complicate relations between the two countries. This book deals with the entire range of problems between the two nations, with major emphasis on the immigration issue and the effects of petroleum exploitation. Such topics discussed are Mexican oil and nationalism, a flood of Mexicans, economic dreams and realities, and the tasks of diplomacy.

21. Sistema Economico Latinamericano/Latin American Economic System. *Latin American-U.S. Economic Relations, 1982–1983.* Boulder, CO: Westview Press, 1984. 119 p.
Many economic decisions are based on the differences of the relationship of the Latin American Economic System (SELA) and that of the United States. In 1981 the Latin American Council established a number of criteria and objectives that Latin American countries should establish and promote in the context of their relations with the United States. Further, it identified a number of important measures relating to trade, commodities, financing, transnational enterprises, foreign investment, and the transfer of technology. The volume begins with a study of the U.S. domestic economic policy followed by an analysis of the international repercussions of this policy. The final chapter reviews the economic relations between Latin America and the United States.

22. Smith, Robert Freeman, ed. *The United States and the Latin American Sphere of Influence. Volume II. Era of Good Neighbors, Cold Warriors, and Hairshirts, 1930–1982.* Malabar, FL: Robert E. Krieger Publishing Company, 1983. 147 p.
This volume disputes the viewpoint that every guerrilla in Latin America spouting Marxist cliches is a saintly savior of the people. It also emphasizes that some Latin countries will develop, others will remain in about the same condition as they are today, and some will become less well developed and that the United States will not have much to do with whatever happens in the future. The book is chronologically developed

from 1930 to 1982. There is an excellent chapter on the economic dimension of the problem from 1945 to 1982.

23. Steward, Dick. *Money, Marines and Missions: Recent U.S.-Latin American Policy.* Lanham, MD: University Press of America, 1980. 280 p.

24. Vasquez, Carlos, and Garcia y Griego, Manuel, eds. *Mexican-U.S. Relations: Conflict and Convergence.* UCLA Chicano Studies Research Center Anthropology No. 3 and UCLA Latin America Center Latin American Studies Vol. 56. Los Angeles: University of California, UCLA Chicano Studies Research Center Publications and UCLA Latin American Center Publications, 1983. 490 p.

This book provides a general introduction to a wide range of issues in Mexico-U.S. relations. It presents several interpretations of contemporary U.S.-Mexican relations. Several essays were chosen to provide concise introductions to key problems in contemporary binational problems and explanations of how these issues are inextricably related. Other aspects are included that address specific problems such as the Mexican petroleum industry and its relation with the United States and the problems of the migrant workers. The sixteen chapters of this volume were written between 1977 and 1982. They provide a variety of viewpoints about the changing political and economic realities of U.S.-Mexican relations.

25. Wesson, Robert G. *The United States and Brazil, Limits of Influence.* Praeger Special Studies. New York: Praeger, 1981. 179 p.

26. Wesson, Robert G., ed. *U.S. Influence in Latin America in the 1980s.* Politics in Latin America, a Hoover Institution Series. New York: Praeger, 1982. 242 p.

This volume develops some ideas regarding the means and magnitude of U.S. influence in Latin America. Ten countries were selected for analysis: Mexico and Cuba for their direct importance as neighbors; Brazil, Colombia, Argentina, and Venezuela for general economic and political importance; Chile because of the controversial nature of its relations with the United States; and Panama, Nicaragua, and El Salvador because of the very large role formerly or currently played by the United States in their political lives. The volume emphasizes the current period. Although each country is different, a fairly coherent picture of the influence of the United States is presented.

27. Wesson, Robert G., and Muñoz, Heraldo, eds. *Latin American Views of U.S. Policy.* Praeger Special Studies. New York: Praeger, 1986. 153 p.

Because of the growing importance of inter-American relations, Latin America has acquired a more salient place in the attention of the United States. While many of the reasons for the expanding relations are disagreeable, such as the narcotic trade and the mountainous debts, there are also welcome developments, such as the increasing share of oil imports from Latin America and the strong trends to democratization. The growing role of the United States in both the political and economic sphere of Latin America is voiced in this volume. The authors are eminent scholars from the countries they discuss.

FOREIGN INVESTMENTS IN LATIN AMERICA

28. Aspe-Armella, Pedro; Dornbusch, Rudiger; and Obstfeld, Maurice, eds. *Financial Policies and the World Capital Market: The Problem of Latin American Countries.* Chicago: University of Chicago Press, 1983. 304 p.

29. Baklanoff, Eric N. *Expropriation of U.S. Investments in Cuba, Mexico and Chile.* Praeger Special Studies in International Economics and Development. New York: Praeger, 1975. 170 p.
This is a study of the uncompensated or insufficiently compensated expropriation of U.S. investments in Latin America. In contrast to nationalization agreements reached through negotiation, this volume is concerned with unilateral state action by which the property of the private owner is taken without the provision of prompt, adequate, and effective compensation. The volume focuses on Mexico, Cuba, and Chile. In each of these nations, changes in internal policy shaped new policies toward foreign-controlled enterprises. The study compares the experiences in each of the three nations, analyzes the impact of U.S.-controlled enterprises on the host nation, and evaluates, in the light of these experiences, U.S. investment policy toward Latin America.

30. Black, Jan K. *United States Penetration of Brazil.* Philadelphia, PA: University of Pennsylvania Press, 1977. 313 p.
This volume is a study analyzing the relationship between the security issue, as conceived by the United States, and the political role of the military in Latin America. The material is focused on Brazil to evaluate why so many U.S. scholars, writing about the 1964 coup d'etat and its aftermath there, ignored what so many Latin American scholars took for granted (but failed to document): U.S. complicity. The processes which have been the focus of this study are those by which the United States has attempted to modify or perpetuate the internal balance of political forces in Brazil.

31. Carl, Beverly M. *A Guide to Incentives for Investing in Brazil.* Dallas, TX: Southern Methodist University Press, 1972. 58 p.
Brazil possesses a dynamic economy that is especially attractive for the potential investor. The volume begins with a general overview of Brazil as an investment site considering the population and labor force, resources, and the state of the economy as to industrialization, investment climate, and economic relations with the Unites States. Regional investment incentives are then analyzed for the Northeast, Amazon, and Espirito Santo. The national incentives are considered with emphasis on the potential for the fishing industry and tourism. A short section is devoted to Brazilian and international sources of credit. Finally, there is an evaluation of United States governmental programs affecting investments in Brazil.

32. Knudsen, Harold. *Expropriation of Foreign Investments in Latin America.* New York: Universitet, 1975. 356 p.

33. Mikesell, Raymond F. *Foreign Investment in Copper Mining: Case Studies of Mines in Peru and Papua New Guinea.* Resources for the Future Series. Baltimore, MD: Johns Hopkins University Press, 1975. 166 p.

34. Moore, John R. *The Impact of Foreign Direct Investment on an Underdeveloped Economy: The Venezuelan Case.* Edited by Stuart Bruchey and Eleanor Bruchey. American Business Abroad Series. Salem, NH: Ayer Co., 1976. 303 p.

35. Peat Marwick Auditores Independentes. *Investment in Brazil.* New York: Peat Marwick Mitchell and Co., 1983. 105 p.

36. Rosenn, Keith, et al. *Regulation of Foreign Investment in Brazil: A Critical Analysis.* Washington, DC: American Enterprise Institute for Public Policy Research, 1983. 65 p.

37. Shea, Donald R. *Reference Manual on Doing Business in Latin America.* 2d ed. Milwaukee, WI: University of Wisconsin-Milwaukee, Center for Latin America, 1980. 210 p.

38. U.S. Department of Commerce. *U.S. Investments in Latin American Economy.* Edited by Stuart Bruchey and Eleanor Bruchey. American Business Abroad Series. Salem, NH: Ayer Co., 1976. 194 p.

39. U.S. Department of Commerce. Bureau of Foreign and Domestic Commerce. *Investments in Latin America and the British West Indies.* Edited by Mira Wilkins. European Business Series: Special Agent 169. Salem, NH: Ayer Co., 1977. 544 p.

40. Winkler, Max. *Investments of United States Capital in the Latin American Economy.* Port Washington, NY: Associated Faculty Press, 1971. 297 p.
This volume presents the evolution of investment in Latin America from the earliest period to the 1920s. As the investment from the United States grew, problems evolved that were unique. Shortly after the turn of the twentieth century the U.S. corporations operating in Latin America came to realize that national good will was an important factor in the success of their undertakings. The way the corporations developed and operated in their early developments is analyzed. The material of this volume provides a background to developments of a later date.

AMERICAN CORPORATIONS IN LATIN AMERICA

41. Bruchey, Stuart, and Bruchey, Eleanor, eds. *The General Electric Company in Brazil.* American Business Abroad Series. National Planning Association, Salem, NH: Ayer Co., 1976. 105 p.

42. Edelberg, Guillermo S. *The Procurement of Practices of the Mexican Affiliates of Selected United States Automobile Firms.* Edited by Stuart Bruchey and Eleanor Bruchey. American Business Abroad Series. Salem, NH: Ayer Co., 1976. 201 p.

43. Montavon, Remy, et al. *The Role of Multinational Companies in Latin America: A Case Study in Mexico.* Praeger Special Studies. New York: Praeger, 1980. 124 p.

ECONOMIC DEVELOPMENT

44. Bolland, O. Nigel. *Belize: A New Nation in Central America.* Westview Profiles—Nations of Contemporary Latin America. Boulder, CO: Westview Press, 1986. 157 p.
This is a profile of one of the newest nations in Latin America. The volume traces the major shifts in the economy that have occurred since World War II including recent developments in consumption patterns, communications, trade unions, and government economic policies. The emergence and culmination of Belize's independence movement are explored in light of the country's internal politics and regional relations with other Commonwealth Caribbean nations and the Central American republics. The book concludes with an evaluation of Belize's problems and an assessment of its prospects for the future.

45. Falcoff, Mark; Grunwald, Joseph; and Wiarda, Howard J. *The Crisis in Latin America, Strategic, Economic, Political Dimensions.* Edited by Howard J. Wiarda. Studies in Foreign Policy. Washington, DC: American Enterprise Institute for Public Policy Research, 1984. 32 p.

46. Gwynne, Robert N. *Industrialisation and Urbanisation in Latin America.* London: Croom Helm, 1985. 259 p.
This is an up-to-date study of industrialization in Latin America. Industry is emphasized rather than cities. A number of themes are analyzed using a wide variety of examples, though emphasis is placed on Chile. The first section reviews the debt crisis and the particular problems of Latin American countries. The second section considers the problem of economic regional integration and the applications of spatial location theory applied to the region's industries. The third section discusses industry in its urban setting. This is a basic analysis of industrial development in Latin America today.

47. Harrison, Lawrence E. *Underdevelopment Is a State of Mind: The Latin American Case.* Lanham, MD: University Press of America, and The Center for International Affairs, Harvard University, 1985. 192 p.
In this volume the basic theme developed is that more than any other of the numerous factors that influence the development of countries is its culture which principally explains, in most cases, why some countries develop more rapidly and equitably than others. By "culture" is meant

the values and attitudes a society inculcates in its people through various socializing mechanisms such as the home, school, and church. The major portion of this book examines the experiences of pairs of countries or regions, most of which started with the same basic resource endowment but have developed very differently. The paired countries are Nicaragua and Costa Rica, Dominican Republic and Haiti, Barbados and Haiti, Argentina and Australia, Spain and Spanish America, and, finally, Spanish America and the United States. The author worked between 1962 and 1982 for the U.S. Agency for International Development (AID).

48. Hill, A. David, ed. *Latin American Development Issues.* Proceedings of the Conference of Latin Americanist Geographers, Syracuse, New York, December 2–4, 1971. Vol. 3. East Lansing, MI: C.L.A.G. Publications, 1971. 203 p.

49. International Bank for Reconstruction and Development/The World Bank. *Brazil: Financial Systems Review.* A World Bank Country Study. Washington, DC, 1984. 160 p.
Brazil's complex financial systems have played a central role in the evolution of its economy over the past two decades. This volume presents a chronological development of the financial changes from the mid-1960s. The volume begins with the financial reforms of the 1960s with an analysis of the financial structures that evolved. The problems of inflation are given attention. The Brazilian financial policy after 1974 was based on four main strands. First, capital inflows were encouraged. Second, credit subsidies increased dramatically. Third, federal debt issue was employed to recycle funds from savings surplus to deficit sectors, and fourth, a restrictive monetary policy was developed.

50. Kim, Kwan S., and Ruccio, David F., eds. *Debt and Development in Latin America.* Notre Dame, IN: University of Notre Dame Press, 1985. 226 p.
In recent years there has been a renewed interest in the United States of economic trends and events in Latin America. This interest is to a large extent the growing awareness of the close interrelationships between the Latin American economies and the U.S. economy. The present interest has been largely triggered by the international debt crisis in Latin America and its possible devastating effect on U.S. banks and more generally on the U.S. economy. This volume discusses not only the current debt situation but some of the structural factors that made Latin American economies vulnerable. A balanced view from different perspectives on the current economic crisis in Latin America is presented.

51. Kowalewski, David. *Transnational Corporations and Caribbean Inequalities.* Praeger Special Studies. New York: Praeger, 1982. 235 p.
A major problem of the twentieth century is the maldistribution of global resources. The growing gap between the privileged and the deprived is an especially salient issue in the Third World. Third World countries are increasingly integrated into the global political economy dominated by transnational corporations and transnational banks. Consequently the global operations of these huge economic entities are being regarded more and more as a significant explanation for Third World inequalities.

This book explores the utility of the theory of Third World intranational inequalities by focusing on the operations of transnational corporations in the islands of the Caribbean Basin. Such aspects are analyzed as transnational class formation; political inequality; economic inequality as to jobs, wages, and occupations; and social inequality.

52. Leiken, Robert S. *Central America: Anatomy of Conflict.* Published in Cooperation with Carnegie Endowment for International Peace. New York: Pergamon Press, 1984. 351 p.
The essays of this volume present a collection of independent works that together represent a cross section of American political opinion from conservative to radical. With political upheaval in the 1970s, Central America became an area that received intense attention in Washington. The Carter administration, unable to find a political solution to the Nicaraguan crisis, acquiesced to the Sandinistas' coming to power. When the Sandinistas embraced Moscow and Havana, the United States government was embarassed. Yet the Reagan administration has had an even more burdensome time. Repeated presidential attempts have not won public backing. This volume has sections on socialism and Sovietism, economic and military realities, and the policy process.

53. Mathis, F. John. *Economic Integration in Latin America.* Studies in Latin American Business: No. 8. Austin, TX: University of Texas, Bureau of Business Research, 1969. 112 p.

54. Montavon, Remy; Wionczek, Miguel; and Piquerez, Francis. *The Role of Multinational Companies in Latin America.* Praeger Special Studies. New York: Praeger, 1980. 113 p.
The presence and operations of multinational corporations in the developing countries are frequently criticized. It is usually admitted that the multinationals wield a decisive influence in a number of developing countries, certainly in the economic field. This volume considers such fundamental questions: Do multinational corporations constitute a factor of economic autonomy or dependency as far as these countries are concerned? Do they or do they not promote economic integration in these countries? Do they meet the development priorities which these countries have selected? Mexico is used as a case study, for since 1972 this Latin American country has been pursuing a coherent policy of economic development, and the government has created a system of industrial and technological policy instruments which define how foreign companies may operate.

55. Newfarmer, Richard S. *Profits, Progress and Poverty: Case Studies of International Industries in Latin America.* Notre Dame, IN: University of Notre Dame Press, 1985. 489 p.
This volume presents a series of case studies of industries in Latin America. An introduction provides background on recent general economic trends and international industrial organization and development. The industries analyzed include the cigarette, iron and steel, electrical, automobile, and food processing. Special implications for Latin American developments are stressed for the tire, pharmaceutical, and tractor industries. The final chapter considers international oligopoly and uneven development in the world. This book provides substantive contribu-

tions and theoretical insights regarding the role of international oligopolies in Latin American industrialization.

56. Rietti, Mario. *Money and Banking in Latin America.* Praeger Special Studies. New York: Praeger, 1979. 295 p.
Latin America's economic and social development reflects the complex nature of a region consisting of countries in various stages of development. In an increasingly interdependent world, the development of economic activity at the national, regional, and international levels is closely linked. It is within this context that this exhaustive analysis of the monetary, financial, and banking systems is presented since the early 1960s. Stress is given to the noteworthy progress made in expediting financial growth, in mobilizing financial resources, and in strengthening savings and investment in the countries of the region. The volume also points out the progress achieved in Latin America in the institutional field, particularly in planning, investments, and financial intermediation.

57. Swift, Jeannine. *Economic Develoment in Latin America.* New York: St. Martin's Press, 1978. 154 p.
This volume provides an introduction to the economies of Latin America. The various issues are viewed from the perspective of problems rooted in the history of each country. Although some of the specificity of strict economic analysis is lost, insights are obtained that are missing when only pure economic variables are used. Such aspects are discussed as models of development, formation of the conditions for underdevelopment, multinational corporations, technology and employment, and inflation in South America.

58. Villegas, J. E. *Brazil as a Model for Developing Countries.* New York: Vantage Press, 1979. 77 p.

59. Wiarda, Howard J., and Kline, Harvey F., eds. *Latin American Politics and Development.* 2d ed. Boulder, CO: Westview Press, 1985. 671 p.
The economic and political life of Latin America is extremely dynamic. This volume places emphasis on the political economy, public policy, and the relations of dependency in which the Latin American nations find themselves. The volume begins with an extensive introduction stressing historical development, acceleration of modernization since 1930, interest groups and political parties, public policy, and the Latin American political process. This is followed by a country-by-country treatment of Latin America. Each of the country chapters emphasizes the particular type of development occurring in that country.

ECONOMIC POLICY

60. Barrett, Jeffrey W. *Impulse to Revolution in Latin America.* Praeger Special Studies. New York: Praeger, 1985. 357 p.
In early 1970 Carlos Rangel Guevara wrote, "Almost five hundred years have elapsed since 1492, half a millenium. If we try to summarize those five centuries of Latin American history . . . the most certain, most

truthful, and most general observation we can make about it is that up to the present day, it has been a story of failure." This theme of national failure is an important one throughout this book. The first part of the volume explores the most conspicuous form of national failure in Latin America, economic underdevelopment, and pays particular attention to the cultural and political factors that have retarded economic growth. The second section considers the great potential that exists in Latin America for totalitarian political solutions.

61. Behrman, Jere R., and Hanson, James A., eds. *Short-Term Macroeconomic Policy in Latin America: Conference on Planning and Short-Term Macroeconomic Policy in Latin America.* National Bureau of Economic Research. Other Conference Series, No. 14. Cambridge, MA: Ballinger Publishing Co., 1979. 416 p.
In 1974 and 1975 the Latin American economies experienced particularly severe inflation. Many of the Central American countries suffered double digit inflation while Chile and Argentina suffered hyperinflation of over 30 percent per month. As a consequence the Panamanian Ministry of Planning and Economic Policy, the Latin American Institute for Economic and Social Planning, and the National Bureau of Economic Research held a conference to examine short-run Latin American macroeconomic policy. The objectives were to evaluate the usefulness of short-run forecasting techniques, to reassess short-run constraints on policymaking, and to consider the impact of conventional monetary and fiscal policy in the Latin American institutional framework.

62. Dominguez, Jorge I., ed. *Mexico's Political Economy, Challenges at Home and Abroad.* Series: Sage Focus Editions, 47. Beverly Hills, CA: Sage Publications, Inc., 1982. 239 p.

63. Grunwald, Joseph, ed. *Latin America and World Economy: A Changing International Order.* Vol. 2, Latin American International Affairs Series. Beverly Hills, CA: Sage Publications, Inc., 1978. 323 p.

64. Karnes, Thomas L., ed. *Readings in the Latin American Policy of the United States.* Tucson, AZ: University of Arizona Press, 1972. 302 p.
This volume, based on historical concepts, provides a collage of essays presenting developments from the earliest settlement of Latin America to the present. There is an emphasis on the relation of the United States to the Latin American countries. Such aspects are stressed as the importance of the Monroe Doctrine and its challenges, Panama as a world highway, dollar diplomacy, and some modern alliances. This volume presents a historical overview of the development of Latin America in relation to the United States.

65. Lincoln, Jennie K., and Ferris, Elizabeth G. *The Dynamics of Latin American Foreign Policies: Challenges for the 1980s.* Westview Special Studies on Latin America and the Caribbean. Boulder, CO: Westview Press, 1984. 325 p.
This volume presents a series of essays on the dynamics of Latin American policies in the 1980s. The first section considers the Latin American

national governments in the international system of states. The attempts at regional integration are stressed. The second part discusses economic challenges and regional conflicts in South America. Part three is devoted to the challenges of revolution in Central America. The final part considers a possible theory for the comparative analysis of Latin American foreign policy. The volume stresses the interrelationships between political and economic decisions.

66. *Methods for Evaluating Latin American Export Operations.* Springfield, VA: Organization of American States, 1978. 113 p.

67. Petras, James F. *Class, State, and Power in the Third World: With Case Studies on Class Conflict in Latin America.* Totowa, NJ: Allanheld, Osmun & Co., 1981. 285 p.

68. Randall, Stephen J. *The Diplomacy of Modernization: Colombian-American Relations, 1920–1940.* Toronto, Canada and Buffalo, NY: University of Toronto Press, 1977. 239 p.
The basic objective of this study is concerned with the relationship between government and private enterprise, the factors which shaped policymaking in both the United States and Colombia, and the nature of the Colombian response to the American presence. In a specialized study of one country, the goal is to understand more fully the nature of what became the Good Neighborhood policy and some of the achievements. The major political personalities are not stressed by other influences that shaped policy. This is a historical study of the period between 1920 and 1940. Such aspects are discussed as finance diplomacy, American enterprise and Colombian petroleum, bananas and politics, and the Scadta phantom.

69. Sosá-Rodriguez, Raul. *Les Problèmes Structurels des Relations Économiques Internationales de l'Amerique Latine.* Études d'Histoire Économique, Politique et Sociale, XLVII. Geneve, Switzerland: Labrairie Droz, 1963. 252 p.

COMMERCE AND TRADE

70. Baer, Werner, and Samuelson, Larry. *Latin America in the Post-Import Substitution Era.* Elmsford, NY: Pergamon Press, 1977. 168 p.

71. Baer, Werner, and Gillis, Malcolm, eds. *Export Diversification and the New Protectionism: The Experience in Latin America.* Champaign, IL: University of Illinois Press, 1981. 301 p.
This volume contains papers and comments of the conference "Trade Prospects Among the Americas: Latin American Export Diversification and New Protectionism" held in 1980 in Sao Paulo, Brazil. The principal focus of the conference was upon trade relations between Latin America and the advanced industrial nations, particularly the United States. In addition opportunities for, and constraints upon, intra-Latin American

trade are examined. Some of the papers in the volume are primarily empirical in character, others focus upon theoretical considerations.

72. Blough, Roy, and Behrman, Jack N. *Regional Integration and the Trade of Latin America.* CED Supplementary Paper No. 22. New York: Committee for Economic Development, 1968. 184 p.
The major emphasis of this book is an analysis of methods by which the economic development of Latin American countries might be accelerated through the integration of national economies into one or more regional groupings. Attempts to accomplish integration such as the establishment of the Latin American Free Trade Area and Central American Common Market have been difficult. This volume discusses the possible origin of the Latin American Common Market proposed by the Latin American presidents in 1970.

73. Business International Corporation. *Profits under Pressure in Latin America: Bottom-Line Strategies for a Changing Market.* New York: August 1985. 175 p.
This volume has been prepared by Business International in order to help companies devise management strategies for Latin America's increasingly volatile economic environment. A practical management tool is provided that uses checklists, cases examples, and diagrams to help executives focus on central issues affecting their operations and to identify the fundamental keys to success. Research for this report is based on more than fifty intensive personal interviews with U.S. and European companies active in Latin America.

74. Business International Corporation. *Trading in Latin America: The Impact of Changing Policies.* New York: July 1981. 237 p.
Latin American countries are restructuring their system of imports and exports. The general trend is to abandon their import substitution policies and open their doors to foreign competition. Each country of Latin America, excluding Central America, is treated separately. Argentina, Chile, and Uruguay illustrate the trend toward dismantling import barriers. Mexico and Peru have launched some import liberalization policies. In contrast, there are still countries, such as Brazil, that maintain stiff export quotas. In virtually all countries substantial changes in trade rules have occurred. Some of these shifts are due to a booming market for imports, problems of local manufacturing operations, changes in the structure of manufacturing, and the new opportunities for exporters.

75. Czinkota, Michael R., ed. *U.S.-Latin American Trade Relations: Issues and Concerns.* New York: Praeger, 1983. 316 p.

76. Diaz-Alejandro, Carlos F. *Foreign Trade Regimes and Economic Development.* Colombia, Bk. 9. Edited by Jagdish N. Bhagivati and Anne O. Krueger. Special Conference Series. Cambridge, MA: National Bureau of Economic Research, 1976. 281 p.

77. Dow, J. Kamal. *Colombia's Foreign Trade and Economic Integration in Latin America.* University of Florida Latin American Monographs: No. 9. Gainesville, FL: University Presses of Florida, 1971. 84 p.

78. Jorge, Antonio; Salazar-Carrillo, Jorge; and Sanchez, Enrique P. *Trade, Debt and Growth in Latin America.* New York: Pergamon Press, 1984. 165 p.
The basic purpose of this book is to explore the inter-relations of the foreign debt with the international trade of the area and its prospects for economic development. It is evident that the issues in question cannot be realistically contemplated in isolation or resolved independently of one another. This volume stresses the theme that there is economic integration of international trade and financial and monetary systems. The developed and underdeveloped world requires close linkages for a strong world trade and a healthy world economy.

79. Longrigg, S. J., ed. *Major Companies of Brazil, Mexico and Venezuela, 1979/1980.* London: Graham and Trotman Ltd., 1979. 405 p.
The major companies of Brazil, Mexico, and Venezuela are listed. Typical information given includes address, telephone and cable numbers, president, directors, principal activities, branch offices, principal banker, subsidiaries, financial information, number of employees, profits, and capital. A number of foreign companies are included that are making a solid contribution to the business environment of Latin America. These companies are largely North American, European, and Japanese.

80. Price Waterhouse and Co. *Doing Business in the Dominican Republic.* New York: 1984. 107 p.

81. Shea, Donald R., et al. *Reference Manual on Doing Business in Latin America.* Milwaukee, WI: University of Wisconsin-Milwaukee, The Center for Latin America, Milwaukee, 1979. 207 p.
This volume has been published to facilitate the conduct of business in Latin America. It provides an evaluative guide to the substantial but widely scattered information and reference material on this subject. The major parts of the volume consider doing business in Latin America, general reference materials, information sources, bibliographic citations, services provided U.S. business by the federal government, Latin American governments, foreign counsels, and private agencies. Selected copies of doing business in Latin America include cross-cultural dimensions, commercial arbitration, joint ventures, private sector capital mobilization, and investment and contract guarantees.

82. Shea, Donald R., and Swacker, Frank W., eds. *Business and Legal Aspects of Latin American Trade and Investment.* Milwaukee, WI: University of Wisconsin-Milwaukee, The Center for Latin America, 1977. 219 p.

83. Sherman, William R. *The Diplomatic and Commercial Relations of the United States and Chile, 1820–1914.* New York: Russell & Russell, 1973. 224 p.
This is a historical study of the diplomatic and commercial relations between the United States and Chile in the nineteenth and early twentieth centuries. Stress is placed on the need for more foreign imports of

materials as industrialization grew in the United States. This volume provides an excellent background to many of the modern-day events.

84. Syrquin, Moshe, ed. *Trade, Stability, Technology and Equity in Latin America.* New York: Academic Press, 1982. 492 p.
While in recent decades there has been substantial economic and social progress in Latin America, income inequality, underemployment of physical and human resources, and external constraints still persist. The various contributions in this book attempt to deal with specific aspects of the recent Latin American economic development process. This book offers a multifaceted, yet detailed, analysis of key issues based on five broad topics of recent concern to specialists: international trade, external instability, stabilization and growth, technology, and equity. Such specific topics considered are balance of payments, pros and cons of external debts, implication of foreign trade, and experiences with the promotion of labor-intensive exports of manufacturers.

85. University of Texas. Lyndon B. Johnson School of Public Affairs. *U.S. Finance and Trade Links with Less-Developed Countries: A Report by the U.S.-LDC Trade Link Policy Research Project, the University of Texas.* Lyndon B. Johnson School of Public Affairs Policy Research Project Report No. 61. Austin, TX, 1984. 116 p.

86. *U.S.-Latin America Trade Relations in the 1980s.* An Executive Summary of an NCEIS Conference. Washington, DC: National Center of Export-Import Studies, 1984. 20 p.

87. Weintraub, Sidney. *Free Trade between Mexico and the United States?* Washington, DC: The Brookings Institution, 1984. 205 p.
For much of the twentieth century, U.S. foreign policy was focused outside the Americas. Beginning in 1973–74 with the world oil crisis and the discovery of huge quantities of oil in Mexico, United States began to develop its trade relationships with Mexico. By the late 1970s, Mexico had become the third-ranking U.S. trading partner after Canada and Japan. This study is an analysis of the possibility that Mexico and the United States can move gradually toward free trade for substantially all goods. It examines the political impediments to such a movement, but it concentrates on economic issues, especially whether the benefits of free trade would be shared equitably or would tend to favor the more advanced U.S. economy.

88. Weintraub, Sidney. *United States-Latin America Trade and Financial Relations: Some Policy Recommendations.* CEPAL Manuals. University of Miami Publications in Economics, No. 5. Coral Gables, FL: University of Miami Press, 1961. 188 p.
This report on the financial and trade relations between the U.S. and less-developed countries is the product of a policy research project conducted by the Lyndon B. Johnson School of Public Affairs of the University of Texas in 1983–84. The material begins with the debt crisis analyzing such aspects as finance and trade links, tools of international finance, mobilizing private capital, and general agreements on tariffs and trade. This is followed by conflicting views on the debt crisis and investment in economic development. The final section provides a sector analysis of the Mexican economy.

TECHNOLOGICAL INNOVATION

89. Baranson, Jack. *North-South Technology Transfer: Financing and Institution Building.* Mt. Airy, MD: Lomond Publications, 1981. 160 p.
This volume addresses the problems of the transfer of technology between the United States and Latin American enterprises. In recent times there has been an ever-widening gap between Latin American demands and the inadequate response of U.S. enterprise groups. The situation is analyzed for Brazil, Colombia, and Mexico. The study stresses the continuing set of issues between the United States and Latin American countries over the international transfer of industrial technology and the U.S. business enterprises involved in Latin American countries. Such aspects considered are the economy and technology, managing technological development, technology support structures, and technology-sharing agreements.

90. Street, James H., and James, Dilmus D., eds. *Technological Progress in Latin America: The Prospectus for Overcoming Dependency.* Westview Special Studies on Latin America and the Caribbean. Boulder, CO: Westview Press, 1979. 257 p.
In the light of the energy crisis and the problems of feeding a rapidly growing and urbanizing population, Latin America faces a critical need to acquire scientific and technological knowledge. While some writers feel that the region is hopelessly dependent on foreign governments and multinational corporations for its technology, the writers of this volume believe that there are internal technological possibliities as demonstrated by concrete instances. The introductory section reviews the nature of technological dependency and makes a case for indigenous research and development. The major portion of the volume is devoted to case studies of successful innovations. These include barriers perceived by Colombian industrialists, technical knowledge available to Mexican farmers, innovations in the pulp and paper industry of Mexico, and multinational firms in Brazil.

PETROLEUM INDUSTRY

91. Baker, George. *Mexico's Petroleum Sector: Performance and Prospect.* Tusla, OK: Penn Well Publishing Company, 1984. 290 p.
The great growth years for the Mexican oil industry were from 1976 to 1982. Since then the glamor role given to oil has disappeared, and the future of the industry cannot be predicted from past experience. It is gradually being recognized that Mexican oil management is a function of Mexican culture and personality no less than of Mexican history and economics. This volume provides a comprehensive picture of the Mexican oil industry. Such aspects discussed are size of the industry, government investments, sales of Pemex, procurement, investment costs and

returns, political management, national policy, and Mexico in its international setting.

92. Meyer, Lorenzo. *Mexico and the United States in the Oil Controversy, 1917-1942.* Translated by Muriel Vasconcellos. Austin, TX: University of Texas Press, 1977. 367 p.
The study of the development of the oil industry in Mexico from its beginnings in the early 1900s up to the time of nationalization offers an opportunity to examine one of these processes at close range. The phenomenon unfolds as Mexico, motivated by change in its internal structure, attempts to diminish its economic dependence by gaining control of the foreign-operated oil industry. The result is a conflict between the United States and Mexico. This study is limited to the oil controversy and came to a conclusion with the signing of the compensation agreement in 1942. This is a comprehensive study that follows the events in a logical, chronological order.

93. Millor, Manuel R. *Mexico's Oil: Catalyst for a New Relationship with the U.S.?* Westview Replica Edition. Boulder, CO: Westview Press, 1982. 267 p.
Analyzing the effects of Mexico's newly flourishing petroleum industry, the volume begins with the evolution of Mexico's oil development and provides a detailed assessment of its socioeconomic, political, and ecological consequences and the Mexican government's current energy policies. Millor argues that, far from representing a clear case of positive growth for Mexico, petroleum could bring about distorted development and increased dependency, resulting in difficult relations with the U.S. If stable relations develop, the U.S. policymakers must recognize the emergence of Mexico as a middle power with autonomous goals. Representing both the U.S. and Mexican points of view this volume provides a better understanding of the significance of oil to Mexican development and the future of U.S.-Mexican relations.

94. Philip, George D. E. *Oil and Politics in Latin America: Nationalist Movements and State Companies.* Cambridge Latin American Studies: No. 40. New York: Cambridge University Press, 1982. 608 p.
The basic purpose of this book is to provide an account of the commercial logic of funding, developing, refining, and marketing oil in Latin America and the political environment in which this has taken place. The book is therefore a history rather than an economic study, but it is nevertheless focused on a particular topic. Essentially it aims to provide an account of the conflict that has been played out within the Latin American oil industry between the claims of international capitalism and the more recent claims of national sovereignty and state control. The book begins with the international dimensions. The second part considers the internal political implications of international oil by focusing on some of the major conflicts. The last part discusses the development of state companies in six key Latin American countries.

95. Rabe, Stephen G. *The Road to OPEC: United States Relations with Venezuela, 1919–1976.* Texas Pan American Series. Austin, TX: University of Texas Press, 1982. 272 p.
The United States and Venezuela have interacted dynamically in the twentieth century. Venezuela has been a prime recipient of U.S. capital, a significant trading partner, and a testing ground for U.S. development and reform programs. The exploitation of Venezuela's petroleum, largely by U.S. companies, has profoundly altered Venezuelan political and economic life. This study focuses on the period between 1919 and 1976, the years the U.S. operated the Venezuelan oil industry. Events are presented within a time framework. Not only are significant bilateral issues examined but Venezuelan-U.S. relations are placed within the context of the Latin American policy of the United States. This investigation provides insight into both the politics of the contemporary energy crisis and the growing split between raw material producers and the developed industrial world.

96. Ronfeldt, David, et al. *Mexico's Petroleum and U.S. Policy: Implications for the 1980s.* Santa Monica, CA: Rand Corporation, 1980. 97 p.

97. Tomasek, Robert D. *United States-Mexican Relations: Blowout of the Mexican Oil Well Ixtoc I.* Hanover, NH: American Universities Field Staff, 1981. 10 p.

98. Velasco S., Jesús-Agustin. *Impacts of Mexican Oil Policy on Economic and Political Development.* Lexington, MA: Lexington Books, D.C. Heath & Company, 1982. 236 p.
Mexico is the quintessential example of a developing country where new-found oil wealth has brought development but also problems. Oil has provided an enormous potential boon to the economy, but it also provided an excuse for avoiding the hard choices required for development. Oil provided immediate revenues, but it also created its own bureaucracy. Oil increased the international importance of Mexico, but it complicated the relations with the United States. This volume analyzes the complex problem created by the growing oil industry from both a national and international viewpoint.

99. Wirth, John D., ed. *Latin American Oil Companies and the Politics of Energy.* Latin American Studies Series. Lincoln, NE: University of Nebraska Press, 1985. 282 p.
When Argentina established the world's first state-owned oil company in 1922, it began a trend which fifty years later has become essentially the worldwide norm. This volume is a study of Latin American national oil companies as to how they control, manage, and exploit natural resources for national ends, in name of the common good. Everywhere in Latin America this fundamental tenet of economic nationalism is progressing. The state companies are thus considered a strategic arm of public policy. The large multinational petroleum companies are now subordinate to the nation wherever they operate.

Periodical Literature

Journals and government publications provide a rich source of literature on the economic policies and developments between the United States and Latin America. A wide variety of topics include the United States-Latin American economic relations, American investment, American corporations in Latin America, and commerce and trade. This list has been limited to material in English. It is organized by topic under which the citations are listed by countries. A number of journals such as *Business America, American Import/Export Bulletin, Caribbean Today, Journal of World Business, American Shipper,* and *International Management,* as well as more general economics and business journals, are of particular value in providing information on economics and business in Latin America. The hearings on the Latin American economy by the U.S. Senate and House of Representatives provide basic information on the development of American governmental policies toward our southern neighbors.

UNITED STATES-LATIN AMERICAN ECONOMIC RELATIONS

Mexico

100. Briggs, Everett E. "The United States and Mexico." *Department of State Bulletin* 81 (July 1981): 4–7.
101. "A Crop Failure That Will Fatten Debt." *Business Week* (December 20, 1982): 37.
102. "Fabricating in the Far East? Mexicana Airlines Says There's a Cheaper Way! [Fabricating or Assembling Products in Mexico]." *American Import/Export Management* 101 (July 1984): 30.
103. Green, Maria del Rosario. "Mexico's Economic Dependence." *Proceedings of the Academy of Political Science* 34 (1) (1981): 104–14.
104. Harrell, L., and Fischer, D. "The 1982 Mexican Peso Devaluation and Border Area Employment." *Monthly Labor Review* 108 (October 1985): 25–32.

105. Madison, Christopher. "Mexico Earns Reagan's Moral Support, but Charity Still Begins at Home: The Administration Is Still Waiting for Mexico to Act, but Mexico May Not Be Prepared to Take the Steps Demanded of It until Its New President Takes Office." *National Journal* 14 (October 30, 1982): 1851–53.

106. "Mexico Development, U.S. Inflation Tied." *Oil and Gas Journal* 77 (December 31, 1979): 40–41.

107. "New Tensions Threaten U.S. Links with Mexico." *Business Week* (May 25, 1981): 56–58+.

108. "New U.S.-Mexican Treaty on Auto Theft Urged [Return of Stolen Vehicles]." *National Underwriter (Property & Casualty Insurance Edition)* 86 (June 18, 1982): 50.

109. Rashish, Myer. "North American Economic Relations [United States Relations with Canada and Mexico: Address]." *Department of State Bulletin* 81 (November 1981): 24–28.

110. Reissner, Will. "Mexico: Economy Plunges into Crisis: United States Uses Collapse of Peso to Force Concessions." *Intercontinental Press* 20 (September 6, 1982): 690–92.

111. Reynolds, Clark W. "The Structure of the Economic Relationship." *Proceedings of the Academy of Political Science* 34 (1) (1981): 125–35.

112. Reynolds, Clark W., and McCleery, R. K. "Modeling U.S.-Mexico Economic Linkages." *American Economic Review* 75 (May 1985): 217–22.

113. Tower, F. J. "Third-Ranking U.S. Partner Shows Economic Strength." *Business America* 3 (July 28, 1980): 51.

114. Weintraub, S. "North American Free Trade." *Challenge* 23 (September/October 1980): 48–51.

Central America

115. United States. House Committee on Foreign Affairs. Subcommittee on Inter-American Affairs. *Assessment of Conditions in Central America: Hearings, April 29–May 20, 1980* (96th Congress, 2d Session). Washington, DC: 1980, 137 p.

Costa Rica

116. "Dangers of Leaning Too Hard on Costa Rica." *Business Week* (September 28, 1981): 30.

Nicaragua

117. Conroy, Michael E. "External Dependence, External Assistance and Economic Aggression against Nicaragua." *Latin American Perspectives* 12 (Spring 1985): 39–67.
118. Cuadrado, J. A. "Nicaragua: Despite Reagan's Aid Cutoff, Bankers Play Ball with Sandinistas." *Multinational Monitor* 2 (May 1981): 22–24.
119. Felton, John. "Sanctions on Nicaragua: A Limited Impact? Less Drastic Than Stops against Cuba, Iran." *Congressional Quarterly Weekly Report* 43 (May 11, 1985): 877.

Caribbean Basin

120. Bhattacharya, Anindya K. "Offshore Banking in the Caribbean by U.S. Commercial Banks; Implications for Government-Business Interaction." *Journal of International Business Studies* 11 (Winter 1980): 37–46.
121. "Bigger Role for Puerto Rico in Plans for Caribbean? Interview with José R. Madera, Administrator, Economic Development Administration, Puerto Rico." *U.S. News* 92 (March 22, 1982): 93–94.
122. "U.S. Economic Policy toward Africa and the Caribbean [Proceedings of TransAfrica's Fourth In-House Policy Seminar, January 1983]." *TransAfrica Forum* 1 (Spring 1983): 42–74.
123. Watson, Hilbourne A. "The Political-Economy of U.S.-Caribbean Relations." *Black Scholar* 11 (January/February 1980): 30–41.
124. Yakovlev, P. "American Neocolonialism's Testing Range in the Caribbean." *International Affairs* (2) (February 1985): 70–76.

Dominican Republic

125. Barovick, R.L. "U.S. Programs Build Commercial Links with Dominican Republic." *Business America* 6 (October 31, 1983): 8–9+.
126. Reagan, Ronald, and Blanco, Salvador Jorge. "Visit of President Salvador Jorge Blanco of the Dominican Republic (Exchanges between President Reagan and President Blanco, April 10, 1984)." *Weekly Compilation of Presidential Documents* 20 (April 16, 1984): 512–14, 519–21.

Cuba

127. Morley, Morris H. "The United States and the Global Economic Blockade of Cuba: A Study in Political Pressures on America's Allies [Forming of Multilateral Coalitions to Enforce Economic Sanctions]." *Canadian Journal of Political Science* 17 (March 1984): 25–48.

128. Zimbalist, Andrew. "Soviet Aid, U.S. Blockade and the Cuban Economy." *ACES (Association for Comparative Economic Studies) Bulletin* 24 (Winter 1983): 137–46.

Latin America

129. "Dollars, Not Censure." *Nation's Business* 71 (March 1983): 60+.

130. Edwards, Sebastian, and Teitel, Simon, eds. "Growth, Reform, and Adjustment: Latin America's Trade and Macroeconomic Policies in the 1970s and 1980s." *Economic Development and Cultural Change* 34 (April 1986): 423–671.

131. Hannon, B. "Latin America's Efforts to Cope with Debt Produce Uneven Growth." *Business America* 9 (March 17, 1986): 17+.

132. Losada, Jorge A. "Letdown at Cancún Widens Global Rift [Results of the Meeting of Developed and Developing Nations, Held in Cancún, Mexico, October 1981: Emphasis on United States-Latin American Relations]." *Latin American Times* 3 (November 1981): 8+.

133. Muñoz, Heraldo. "The Strategic Dependency of the Centers and the Economic Importance of the Latin American Periphery [Overall Economic Importance of Latin America for the United States and Other Powers]." *Latin American Research Review* 16 (3) (1981): 3–29.

134. Sheahan, J. "Market-Oriented Economic Policies and Political Repression in Latin America." *Economic Development and Cultural Change* 28 (January 1980): 267–91.

135. United States. House Committee on Foreign Affairs. *Latin America in the World Economy: Hearings, June 15–July 21, 1983, before the Subcommittees on International Economic Policy and Trade and on Western Hemisphere Affairs* (98th Congress, 1st Session). Washington, DC: 1983. 296 p.

136. United States. House Committee on Foreign Affairs. Subcommittee on Inter-American Affairs. *Future Development Assistance to Transitional Countries: Hearings, February 21 and July 23, 1980* (96th Congress, 2d Session). Washington, DC: 1980. 76 p.

137. Wiarda, Howard J., and Perfit, Janine T. eds. *Trade, Aid, and U.S. Economic Policy in Latin America.* Occasional Papers Series, American Enterprise Institute for Public Policy Research, Center for Hemispheric Studies, No. 6. Washington, DC: American Enterprise Institute for Public Policy Research, Center for Hemispheric Studies, 1983. 81 p.

Argentina

138. Acevedo, Domingo E. "The U.S. Measures against Argentina Resulting from Malvinas Conflict [Legal Issues Related to Economic Sanctions against Argentina]." *American Journal of International Law* 78 (April 1984): 323–44.

139. "Backing Britain in Falklands; What Next? The Decision to Come off the Fence Is a Signal to Argentina and U.S. Allies." *U.S. News* 92 (May 10, 1982): 26–28.

140. United States. Senate Committee on Banking, Housing, and Urban Affairs. Subcommittee on International Finance and Monetary Policy. *The Argentinian Debt: Hearing, May 3, 1984, on Details and Implications of U.S. Government Involvement in Both the Argentinian and the Larger Latin American Debt Crises* (Senate Hearing 98–782). Washington, DC: 1984. 108 p.

141. "Why U.S. and Russia Woo Ailing Argentina." *U.S. News* 91 (October 26, 1981): 51–52.

Brazil

142. "Economy Continues Firm but Some Slowing down Probable: Stringent Import Policies Continue to Limit Sales Prospects." *Business America* 3 (December 1, 1980): 24–25+.

143. Garges, L., and Johnson, T. "Fast Pace of U.S. Exports Expected to Slow in 1981." *Business America* 4 (February 9, 1981): 50.

144. Hurrell, Andrew. "Brazil, the United States and the Debt." *World Today* 41 (March 1985): 62–64.

145. Levinson, Marc. "What to Do about Brazil Inc. [A Major Exporter of Everything from Alcohol to Carbon Steel, Much of It Destined for the American Market, Brazil Has Sharply Restricted Imports, Both to Protect Domestic Industries and to Assure a Balance-of-Payments Surplus Sufficient to Cover Interest Payments on Foreign Debt]." *Across the Board* 22 (March 1985): 40–46.

146. Newquist, R. "Protocols with Brazil May Lead to $150 Million in U.S. Exports." *Business America* 7 (April 16, 1984): 20–21.

147. Olson, R. S. "Expropriation and Economic Coercion in World Politics: A Retrospective Look at Brazil in the 1960s." *Journal of Developing Areas* 13 (April 1979): 247–62.

Chile

148. United States. House Committee on Foreign Affairs. *U.S. Economic Sanctions against Chile: Hearing, March 10, 1981, before the Subcommittees on International Economic Policy and Trade and on Inter-American Affairs* (97th Congress, 1st Session). Washington, DC: 1981. 86 p.

AMERICAN INVESTMENT

Mexico

149. Aviel, D., and Aviel, J. B. "American Investments in Mexico." *Management International Review* 22 (1) (1982): 83–96.
150. "Avon: Replacing Imports with Local Supplies." *Institutional Investor* 17 (October 1983): 291.
151. Baerresen, Donald W. "Mexico's Assembly Program: Implications for the United States [Typically, the Labor-Intensive Portions of a Twin Plant Operation Occur in Mexico, while the Capital-Intensive Portions Are Conducted in the United States]." *Texas Business Review* 55 (November/December 1981): 253–57.
152. "Cheap Peso Cuts Cost at Mexican Border." *Electronic Business* 8 (November 1982): 30–31+.
153. Connor, John M., and Mueller, Willard F. "Market Structure and Performance of U.S. Multinationals in Brazil and Mexico." *Journal of Development Studies* 18 (April 1982): 329–53.
154. Ellsworth, David G. "There's More Than Oil: Mexico's Booming Real Estate Industry: U.S. Citizens Reap Benefits from Learning to Cope with Mexico's Foreign Investment Law." *Real Estate Review* 11 (Spring 1981): 129–38.
155. "Ford's Better Idea South of the Border [Building a Small Car Assembly Plant in Hermosillo]." *Business Week* (January 23, 1984): 3–4.
156. Garnier, G., et al. "Autonomy of the Mexican Affiliates of U.S. Multinational Corporations." *Journal of World Business* 14 (Spring 1979): 78–90.
157. "General Foods: Nimbly Pursuing Peso Loans." *Institutional Investor* 17 (October 1983): 284+.

158. Lopez, D. "Eaton Expands South American Output." *Automotive News* (June 30, 1980): E16.

159. Mutter, J. "American Publishers Suffer from Mexican Peso Plunge." *Publishers Weekly* 223 (January 28, 1983): 29–30+.

160. Nossiter, D. D. "Southern Exposure: Totting up the Damages in Mexico." *Barron's* 62 (September 20, 1982): 42–43+.

161. Stevens, D. W. "In the Grip of the Mexican Madness." *Fortune* 106 (November 1, 1982): 131–32+.

162. Stuart, Alexander. "Opportunity Knocks in Troubled Mexico: U.S. Companies Keep Investing in New Ventures, Counting on Tough Austerity Measures to Bring an Economic Revival." *Fortune* 106 (August 23, 1982): 146–48+.

163. Turner, R. J. A. "Mexico Seminar Responds to Commercial Issues Facing U.S. Suppliers and Investors in Mexico." *Business America* 6 (March 7, 1983): 14–15.

164. Winter, D. "Still Cheap but No Longer Third-Rate, Mexico Nears Automotive Bigtime." *Ward's Automotive World* 20 (August 1984): 23–25+.

UNITED STATES-LATIN AMERICAN ECONOMIC DEVELOPMENT

Mexico

165. "Mexico Rattles the Multinationals." *Business Week* (October 4, 1982): 87.

166. "New Interest in Mexican Plants." *Industry Week* 201 (April 16, 1979): 42–43.

167. "1981: The In-Bond Industry Stands Firm [American Owned or Affiliated Assembly Plants in Mexico's Border Cities and Regions]." *Economic Panorama Bancomer* 31 (May 1981): 117–37; (June 1981): 149–58.

168. "Rapid Economic Growth Strains the Country's Resources, Creating Additional Opportunities for U.S. Entrepreneurs." *Business America* 4 (April 6, 1981): 8–10.

169. "The Ripples from Mexico Are Crossing the Rio Grande." *Economist* 285 (November 20, 1982): 67–68.

170. "Why an IBM PC Plant Is Stalled at the Border." *Business Week* (August 6, 1984): 35.

Central America

171. "Business and Revolution in Central America Emphasizes the Influence of American Businesses on the Region's Politics." *Multinational Monitor* 2 (May 1981): Entire Issue.
172. Petras, James F., and Morley, Morris H. "Economic Expansion, Political Crisis and U.S. Policy in Central America." *Contemporary Marxism* (Summer 1981): 69–88.

Guatemala

173. Nairn, Allan. "Guatemala: The Region's Blue Chip Investment Thanks to a Special Relationship between the Ruling Elite and Multinationals." *Multinational Monitor* 2 (May 1981): 12–14.

Nicaragua

174. "A Warmer Welcome for U.S. Businessmen." *Business Week* (January 10, 1983): 43.

Caribbean Basin

175. "Caribbean Investment: Following the Flag? An Interview with Peter Johnson [Executive Director of Caribbean/Central American Action]." *Multinational Monitor* 1 (November 1980): 12–17.
176. Clasen, Thomas F. "The Caribbean Basin Economic Recovery Act and Its Implications for Foreign Private Investment." *New York University Journal of International Law and Politics* 16 (Spring 1984): 715–48.
177. Hughes, A. H. "CBI: New Opportunities for American Business." *Business America* 6 (August 8, 1983): 3–5.
178. Neville, Mark K., Jr., and Rachlin, Lauren D. "Why Corporate Clients Are Moving Offshore to the Caribbean Basin." *New York State Bar Journal* 55 (May 1983): 22–29.
179. Sassen-Koob, S. "Direct Foreign Investment: A Migration Push-Factor? [Impact of U.S. Investment in Export Manufacturing Industries in Southeast Asia and the Caribbean Region on Labor Migration from Those Countries to the U.S.]." *Government and Policy* 2 (4) (1984): 399–416.

180. United States. Department of the Treasury. *Tax Havens in the Caribbean Basin.* Washington, DC: Superintendent of Documents, 1984. 52 p.
181. "U.S. Government Services to Help Businesses Find CBI Opportunities." *Business America* 6 (August 8, 1983): 9–10.

Dominican Republic

182. "Country Continues to Offer Good Opportunities for U.S. Trade and Investment Despite Its Serious Economic Woes." *Business America* 7 (October 15, 1984): 33–35.

Haiti

183. "Improved Economy, CBI Entice Trade, Investment." *Business America* 8 (April 1, 1985): 28–29.
184. Kelly, A. R. "Baseball, Hot Dogs, Apple Pie and Haiti [MacGregor]." *American Import/Export Management* 102 (February 1985): 48–49.

South America

185. Holden, Robert H. "Corporate Officials Embrace Latin Dictators at Private Chamber of Commerce Session [Summary of Discussions at Twelfth Annual Corporate Briefing Session, New York, N.Y.]." *Multinational Monitor* 3 (June 1982): 12–15.
186. Nelson-Horchler, J., and Mazzone, J. "South America: Still a Good Bet?" *Industry Week* 218 (August 22, 1983): 31–34+.
187. "Roundtable: The International Acquisition Market [Panel Discussion]." *Mergers & Acquisitions* 19 (Spring 1984): 26–28+.
188. Sender, H. "What to Do about Blocked Funds." *Dun's Business Month* 123 (June 1984): 74–75+.

Brazil

189. "Brazil: A Billion-Dollar Dream Goes on the Block [Jari]." *Business Week* (January 25, 1982): 41.
190. "Brazil: Public Hostility for a Private Fief [D. Ludwig]." *Economist* 276 (September 27, 1980): 100–01.

191. Caswell, Daniel P. "The Promised Land: Analysis of Environmental Factors of United States Investment in and Development of the Amazon Region in Brazil." *Northwestern Journal of International Law and Business* 4 (Autumn 1982): 517–50.

192. Connor, John M., and Mueller, Willard F. "Market Structure and Performance of U.S. Multinationals in Brazil and Mexico." *Journal of Development Studies* 18 (April 1982): 329–53.

193. "CPC International: Resting Easy on a Large Capital Base." *Institutional Investor* 17 (October 1983): 283–84.

194. Gall, N. "Ludwig's Amazon Empire." *Forbes* 123 (May 14, 1979): 127–30+.

195. "Goodyear: Reaping the Rewards of an Export Agreement." *Institutional Investor* 17 (October 1983): 289+.

196. "How Foreign Banks Still Get Rich in Brazil [Investing in Real Estate to Shelter Local-Currency Loan Profits]." *Business Week* (August 22, 1983): 102.

197. McClenahen, J. S. "Brazil's Confused Economic Outlook." *Industry Week* 207 (November 24, 1980): 77–78+.

198. Rowland, Walter S. "Foreign Investment in Brazil: A Reconciliation of Perspectives [Difficulties a United States Corporation Faces in a Technology Transfer]." *Journal of International Law and Economics* 14 (1) (1979): 39–62.

199. "Signs of Economic Recovery Point to Increased Prospects for American Investments and Exports in Selected Sectors." *Business America* 8 (July 22, 1985): 22–23.

200. Taylor, F. "Sound Management at Last for a Jungle Dream Turned Nightmare [Jari]." *International Management* 39 (January 1984): 24–26.

Ecuador

201. "Ecuador Opens Door to U.S. Investment." *Business America* 8 (April 15, 1985): 29–30.

202. Velocci, A., Jr. "Ecuador Is First Andean Pact Member to Sign OPIC (Overseas Private Investment Corporation) Investment Agreement." *Business America* 8 (April 15, 1985): 31.

Peru

203. Ryser, J., and Robbins, C. A. "Garcia Dusts off an Old Ploy: Expropriation [Nationalization of Belco Petroleum]." *Business Week* (January 13, 1986): 50.

Uruguay

204. "OPIC Mission Will Explore Investment Market in Uruguay." *Business America* 7 (April 16, 1984): 36–37.

AMERICAN CORPORATIONS

Mexico

205. Baldwin, L. "IBM Modifies Proposal for Mexican PC Plant." *Electronic News* 31 (March 18, 1985): 22.
206. Baldwin, L. "Marketers in Mexico Face Money Bind." *Advertising Age* 53 (December 13, 1982): 12.
207. Bamford, J. "Mexican Mirage [Peso Devaluation Creates Currency Translation Problems]." *Forbes* 131 (February 28, 1983): 46.
208. "A Bitter Pill for Drug Multinationals [Import Cutting by Mexico Companies]." *Business Week* (April 30, 1984): 51+.
209. Buchanan, R., and Edid, M. "Revving up for a Run at the U.S. Auto Market." *Business Week* (March 18, 1985): 46.
210. Callahan, J. M. "Mexican Auto Industry—Working with Our Neighbors." *Automotive Industries* 161 (August 1981): 59–61.
211. Carter, C. "Mexico: Newest Market for U.S. Retailers." *Chain Store Age Executive* 57 (November 1981): 37–39.
212. DePrima, A. E. "Border Business Booming." *American Import/Export Management* 96 (February 1982): 20.
213. "Fabricating in the Far East? Mexicana Airlines Says There's a Cheaper Way! [Fabricating or Assembling Products in Mexico]." *American Import/Export Management* 101 (July 1984): 30.
214. "Firms Holding Fast in Mexican Crisis [Currency Devaluation]." *Engineering News-Record* 209 (September 23, 1982): 176.
215. "Ford Pledges to Stay in Cleveland, but Mexico Engine Plant Is Still a Possibility." *Automotive News* (March 3, 1980): 2+.
216. "Ford's Better Idea South of the Border [Building a Small Car Assembly Plant in Hermosillo]." *Business Week* (January 23, 1984): 43–44.
217. Garnier, G., et al. "Autonomy of the Mexican Affiliates of U.S. Multinational Corporations." *Columbia Journal of World Business* 14 (Spring 1979): 78–90.
218. "Jewel Cos: Scoring in Mexico with U.S. Supermarket Techniques." *Business Week* (October 22, 1979): 120+.

219. "Luring Assembly Plants to Mexico." *Industry Week* 204 (February 4, 1980): 30–31.

220. McLean, R. C. "Credit South of the Border." *Credit and Financial Management* 83 (July/August 1981): 44.

221. "Mexico: Auto Makers Flock to a Surging Market." *Business Week* (July 2, 1979): 32–33.

222. "Mexico: A Tough Market to Crack, But." *Engineering News-Record* 206 (June 4, 1981): 30–31.

223. "Mexico: U.S. Computer Makers Rush to Set up Plants." *Business Week* (May 17, 1982): 45.

224. "Mexico: U.S. Drugmakers May Have to Take a Powder." *Business Week* (November 29, 1982): 49+.

225. "Mexico's Devaluation Hurts U.S. Subsidiaries." *Chemical Week* 131 (September 1, 1982): 17–18.

226. Nelson, C. A. "Manufacturing in Mexico Using a Maquiladora [Complimentary Assembly Facility]." *American Import/Export Management* 102 (April 1985): 66+.

227. Rohan, T. M. "Auto Plants Sprout in the Mexican Sun." *Industry Week* 205 (May 12, 1980): 51–53+.

228. Rohan, T. M. "Border-Plant Bonanza Benefiting U.S., Too." *Industry Week* 209 (May 4, 1981): 32+.

229. Rohan, T. M. "Peso Problems Plague U.S. Firms in Mexico." *Industry Week* 216 (January 24, 1983): 20–21.

230. Russell, J. W. "U.S. Sweatshops across the Rio Grande." *Business and Society Review* (50) (Summer 1984): 17–20.

231. Turner, R. "Mexico Turns to Its In-Bond Industry as a Means of Generating Exchange." *Business America* 6 (November 28, 1983): 27–33.

232. Turner, R. "Mexico's In-Bond Industry Continues Its Dynamic Growth." *Business America* 7 (November 26, 1984): 26–30.

233. "U.S. Computer Makers Are Feeling at Home [Assembling Plants in Mexico]." *Business Week* (November 14, 1983): 64.

234. "What Made Apple Seek Safety in Numbers." *Business Week* (March 12, 1984): 42.

235. Whitt, J. D. "Motivating Lower-Level Management of Mexican Affiliates." *Management Accounting* 60 (June 1979): 46–49.

Central America

236. "United Brands: It's Still Mañana for Getting off the Banana Boat." *Business Week* (August 10, 1981): 88–90.

El Salvador

237. Chase, D. "Bullet-Proof Vans, Gun-Toting Chauffeurs Typify Ad Operations." *Advertising Age* 53 (sec. 2) (July 5, 1982): M6.
238. McLeod, D. "Firm Fights Insurer, Brokers over Seized Salvadoran Plant." *Business Insurance* 18 (September 24, 1984): 2+.

Honduras

239. Street, Annie. "Worker Co-Op in Honduras: Women Respond to Corporate Flight [Takeover of a Foundation Garment Factory Closed by Its United States Parent Company, May 1983]." *Dollars and Sense* (January/February 1985): 15–17.

Nicaragua

240. Boyd, L., et al. "The Nicaragua Embargo: Multinationals Aren't Packing." *Business Week* (May 20, 1985): 66.
241. "Nicaragua: A Banana Deal That May Signal a Softer Line." *Business Week* (February 16, 1981): 38.
242. Street, Annie. "El Caso Pennwalt: Mercury Pollution in Nicaragua." *Business and Society Review* 40 (Winter 1981/82): 21–23.

Panama

243. Boyer, E. "Corporate Border Crossers [McDermott International, Inspiration Resources, Lafarge]." *Fortune* 109 (April 30, 1984): 332.
244. Greene, R. "Pack up Your Care and Woe [Relocating in Panama]." *Forbes* 131 (January 17, 1983): 46.

Caribbean Basin

245. "A Caribbean Basin Success Story [Harowe Servo Controls]." *Business America* 6 (August 8, 1983): 12–13.
246. Desrochers, B. "CBI Attracts Investment, Boasts Trade with U.S." *Business America* 8 (March 4, 1985): 40–41.
247. "Five Successful Caribbean Basin Ventures." *Business America* 8 (January 7, 1985): 14.

248. Kane, J. T. "Generating Homegrown Industry and Trade in the Caribbean." *Handling & Shipping Management* 25 (July 1985): 54–56+.

249. "Operating Costs for Free Zones in the Caribbean Basin." *Business Ameirca* 6 (July 25, 1983): 11–15.

250. Sachs, R. T. "Should You Send Your Input Overseas? [Low Cost of Labor Makes the Caribbean Region Attractive for Data Entry Projects]." *Office Administration and Automation* 44 (March 1983): 70–74.

251. "Twin Planting in the Caribbean; Twin Plants in Operation Now." *Business America* 8 (November 25, 1985): 10–11.

252. Wylie, S. "CBI: One Year Later [Caribbean Basin Initiative]." *Business America* 8 (January 7, 1985): 2–5.

Bahamas

253. Roper, L. C. "The Bahamas Becomes CBI's Newest Member [Caribbean Basin Initiative]." *Business America* 8 (April 29, 1985): 26–27.

Dominican Republic

254. Nelson-Horchler, J. "Gulf & Western: Setting an Example." *Industry Week* 217 (April 18, 1983): 36–37.

255. Nelson-Horchler, J. "Social Issues: G & W Says Adios [Gulf & Western Sale of Operations in Dominican Republic]." *Industry Week* 224 (January 21, 1985): 21–23.

Haiti

256. Ebert-Miner, Allan. "How Rawlings [Sporting Goods Co.] Uses Haitian Women to Spin Profits off U.S. Baseball Sales." *Multinational Monitor* 3 (August 1982): 11–12.

257. "Haiti Is Becoming Popular Site for Assembly, Manufacturing." *Business America* 7 (July 23, 1984): 15–17.

Puerto Rico

258. Bray, H. "Puerto Rico's One Note Samba [No Corporate Taxation]." *Across the Board* 22 (January 1985): 3–4.

259. Greene, R. "Drug Abuse [Puerto Rican Tax Shelter]." *Forbes* 130 (August 16, 1982): 36.

260. Hernandez, R. "Puerto Rico Supports Trade and Investment in the Caribbean." *Business America* 8 (January 7, 1985): 10–11.

261. "Ideal Second Home for American Business: Puerto Rico." *Forbes* 126 (November 10, 1980): 201–20.

262. "Living with Lower Incentives." *Business Week* (November 22, 1982): 69.

263. Lurie, M. "Puerto Rico: Problems in Paradise [Special Report]." *Chemical Week* 124 (April 11, 1979): 56–67.

264. Maldonada, A. W. "Recession Hits the Pillmakers' Paradise." *Fortune* 108 (July 25, 1983): 62.

265. "Proposed Section 936 Repeal Is Seen Serious Threat to Caribbean Future [IRS Code Permits U.S. Corporations to Take Tax Credits against Dividends Paid by Corporate Sources in Puerto Rico]." *Handling & Shipping Management* 26 (July 1985): 58.

Virgin Islands

266. "Hess Resumes Output of Benzene and Toulene at Virgin Islands Plant." *Chemical Marketing Reporter* 227 (April 29, 1985): 7+.

Latin America

267. "Come Join Us in Latin America, Says Ford." *Iron Age* 224 (August 24, 1981): 19.

268. Grosse, R. "Regional Offices in Multinational Enterprise: The Latin America Case." *Management International Review* 21 (February 1981): 48–56.

269. "How the Debt Crisis Is Battering Multinationals [Third World Subsidiaries]." *Business Week* (July 25, 1983): 64–66.

270. Sender, H. "What to Do about Blocked Funds." *Dun's Business Monthly* 123 (June 1984): 74–75+.

271. Smith, A. "How to Profit in Latin America." *Euromoney* (January 1984): 93+.

Argentina

272. "Argentine Gains for McCann." *Advertising Age* 53 (August 2, 1982): 48.

Brazil

273. "American Banks: The Booty from Brazil [Businesses inside Brazil]." *Economist* 291 (May 5, 1984): 89–90.
274. Barrett, E., and Cormack, M. P. "How the Brazilian Subsidiary of a U.S. Multinational Reduced Its Exposure to Exchange Losses." *International Management* 40 (April 1985): 83–85.
275. "Brazil: A Bigger Market Slice for U.S. Computers." *Business Week* (November 3, 1980): 55+.
276. "Brazil: Campbell Soup Fails to Make It to the Table." *Business Week* (October 12, 1981): 66.
277. "Brazil Forcing out Foreigners." *Engineering News-Record* 209 (August 26, 1982): 26.
278. "Brazil: A Frustrated ITT Quits a Hot Market." *Business Week* (November 2, 1981): 67.
279. "Brazil: Gerber Abandons a Baby-Food Market." *Business Week* (February 8, 1982): 45+.
280. "Brazil: Local Industry Stops a Big Dow Expansion." *Business Week* (August 25, 1980): 46.
281. "Dow Expansion Bid for Petrochemical Plants Is Rejected by Brazil [Dow Quimica]." *Chemical Marketing Reporter* 217 (June 30, 1980): 3+.
282. "Financier's Dreams May Go down the Drain [Jari's D. K. Ludwig]." *Chemical Week* 128 (March 4, 1981): 18.
283. "Improving Risk Contract Terms Draw More Foreign Companies [Oil Exploration Projects]." *Brazilian Business* 60 (June/July 1980): 30+.
284. Nelson-Horchler, J. "Manville Corp.: A Community's Lifeblood." *Industry Week* 217 (April 18, 1983): 39.
285. Rose, M. M. "Codfish Mission to Brazil Finds Seafood Industry Receptive to U.S. Business." *Business America* 7 (July 23, 1984): 18–21.
286. "Sperry and CDC Move to Strengthen Their Competitive Stance in Brazil." *Data Communications* 13 (September 1984): 64+.
287. "Tough Choices in Brazil: As the Junta Squeezes High-Tech Multinationals More U.S. Companies See Gold as a Hedge." *Business Week* (December 19, 1983): 44–45.

288. Troxell, T. N., Jr. "Woe Is Borden? Not at All: Absent Another Currency Fiasco, It Could Net $5 a Share." *Barron's* 60 (February 18, 1980): 45–46.
289. Wentz, L. "Grey Changes Stir up Drama in Brazil." *Advertising Age* 53 (November 1, 1982): 49.
290. Wentz, L. "Marketing Errors Doomed Sears in Brazil." *Advertising Age* 54 (May 16, 1983): 32.
291. "Why Sears Is Packing It in." *Business Week* (May 9, 1983): 44–45.

Chile

292. "Dow's Chile Strategy Is Paying Off." *Chemical Week* 126 (February 27, 1980): 29–30.

Colombia

293. "Colombian Government Wary of U.S.-Based Coal Firms." *Coal Age* 87 (December 1982): 31.
294. "Quaker Oats Tries Protein Supplement in Colombia." *Food Development* 15 (June 1981): 34+.

Venezuela

295. "Venezuela: No Longer a Preserve of U.S. Companies." *Business Week* (July 23, 1979): 75+.

ECONOMIC ASSISTANCE

Caribbean Basin

296. "Background on the Caribbean Basin Initiative [Includes Summaries of the Economic Situation in the Nations Involved]." *Department of State Bulletin* 82 (April 1982): 7–32.
297. Best, T. "Caribbean Basin Market." *Advertising World* 11 (September 1984): 23–24.
298. "The Caribbean Basin Initiative [Announced by President Reagan, February 24, 1982; Six Articles]." *Foreign Policy* (47) (Summer 1982): 114–38.

299. "Caribbean Basin Initiative: Message to the Congress [March 17, 1982], Transmitting the Proposed Caribbean Basin Economic Recovery Act." *Weekly Compilation of Presidential Documents* 18 (March 22, 1982): 323–27.

300. "Caribbean Basinful of Woes." *Economist* 283 (April 17, 1982): 56.

301. "Caribbean: Corporate Misgivings about U.S. Aid Plans." *Business Week* (April 5, 1982): 40+.

302. "Caribbean: Guns or Butter?" *Economist* 280 (July 18, 1981): 37–38.

303. "CBI [Caribbean Basin Initiaitve] Bill Gets Senate Support." *Business America* 6 (May 2, 1983): 31.

304. "CBI Designation Teams Find Governments and Private Sectors Ready for Business." *Business America* 6 (October 17, 1983): 14–15.

305. "CBI Is Wary of Reagan's Caribbean Initiative." *Chemical Week* 130 (March 3, 1982): 17–18.

306. Charnovitz, S. "Caribbean Basin Initiative: Setting Labor Standards." *Monthly Labor Review* 107 (November 1984): 54–56.

307. Clasen, Thomas F. "The Caribbean Basin Economic Recovery Act and Its Implications for Foreign Private Investment." *New York University Journal of International Law and Politics* 16 (Spring 1984): 715–48.

308. Enders, Thomas O. "A Comprehensive Strategy for the Caribbean Basin: The U.S. and Her Neighbors." *Caribbean Review* 11 (Spring 1982): 10–13.

309. Feinberg, Richard E., et al. "The Battle over the CBI [Caribbean Basin Initiative]: The Debate in Washington." *Caribbean Review* 12 (Spring 1983): 15–18+.

310. Felton, John. "Caribbean Basin Proposal Faces Lengthy Hearings: Numerous Objections Cited [President Reagan's Proposed Package of Foreign Aid, Tax and Trade Benefits]." *Congressional Quarterly Weekly Report* 40 (March 27, 1982): 681–84.

311. Felton, John. "Three House Panels Reject Key Parts of Caribbean Plan [President Reagan's Proposed Caribbean Basin Initiative]." *Congressional Quarterly Weekly Report* 40 (May 15, 1982): 1135.

312. Fitch, G. "CBI Expected to Boost Trade and Development." *Business America* 6 (August 22, 1983): 9–10.

313. Flint, J. "Help!" *Forbes* 126 (December 22, 1980): 29–30.

314. Gonzalez, Heliodoro. "The Caribbean Basin Initiative: Toward a Permanent Dole." *Inter-American Economic Affairs* 36 (Summer 1982): 23–59.

315. Kanchuger, R. "The Caribbean Group." *Finance & Development* 21 (September 1984): 44–46.

316. Knowles, Yareth K., and Bonhomme, Myrtho. "The CBI: A Debate [Caribbean Basin Initiative: Argument I, A Package of Cautious Merit, by Yareth K. Knowles: Argument II, A Missing Point, by Myrtho Bonhomme]." *Migration Today* 10 (5) (1982): 15–21.

317. Kryzanek, Michael J. "President Reagan's Caribbean Basin Formula." *AEI (American Enterprise Institute) Foreign Policy and Defense Review* 4 (2) (1982): 29–36.

318. Lawson, Stanley J., and Flowers, Edward B. "The Caribbean Economy and the Caribbean Basin Initiative: An Introduction." *Review of Business (St. John's University)* 5 (Spring 1984): 3–9.

319. McColm, B. "The Sun Is Setting on Reagan's Caribbean Initiative [Caribbean Basin Initiative]." *Business Week* (December 27, 1982): 42+.

320. Madison, Christopher. "Caribbean Plan Aimed at Keeping Other Nations from Going El Salvador's Way: Though Prompted by the Turmoil in El Salvador, President Reagan's Initiative Primarily Offers Economic Solutions to Social, Political and Military Problems." *National Journal* 14 (March 13, 1982): 459–61.

321. Middendorf, J. William, II. "Programs Underway for the Caribbean Basin Initiative [Programs That Began under Authority of Existing Legislation]." *Department of State Bulletin* 83 (February 1983): 79–83.

322. Montoulieu, C. F. "Caribbean Basin Initiative Should Induce Increased Economic Activity in Puerto Rico." *Business America* 5 (November 29, 1982): 32–33.

323. Organization of American States. Department of Economic Affairs. Special Committee for Consultation and Negotiation. *The United States Generalized System of Preferences; Caribbean Basin Initiative; Coverage and Administrative Procedures in Force in 1984.* Washington, DC: 1984. 77 p.

324. Pastor, Robert A. "Sinking in the Caribbean Basin [Analysis of President Reagan's Caribbean Basin Initiative]." *Foreign Affairs* 60 (Summer 1982): 1038–58.

325. Pastor, Robert A., and Feinberg, Richard. *U.S. Latin American Policy: A Marshall Plan for the Caribbean?* Washington, CT: Center for Information on America, 1984. 6 p.

326. Patureau, Alan. "Tuna Industry Periled by CBI [Caribbean Basin Initiative]." *Puerto Rico Business Review* 7 (June 1982): 2–4.

327. Ramsaran, Ramesh. "The U.S. Caribbean Basin Initiative." *World Today* 38 (November 1982): 430–36.

328. Raymond, Nicholas. "Caribbean Basin Revisited [First Year Results of President Reagan's Caribbean Basin Initiative]." *Editorial Research Reports* (February 1, 1985): 83–100.

329. "The Reagan 'Caribbean Basin Initiative': Pro & Con." *Congressional Digest* 62 (March 1983): 69–96.

330. Reagan, Ronald. "Caribbean Basin Initiative: Address [February 24, 1982] before the Permanent Council of the Organization of American States." *Weekly Compilation of Presidential Documents* 18 (March 1, 1982): 217–25.

331. Reagan, Ronald. "Caribbean Basin Initiative: Remarks [April 28, 1982] at a White House Briefing for Chief Executive Officers of U.S. Corporations." *Weekly Compilation of Presidential Documents* 18 (May 3, 1982): 540–43.

332. "Reagan's Blueprint: The President's Goal Is to Keep Marxist Dictatorships out of the Hemisphere with a Blend of Economic Aid and Military Arms." *U.S. News* 92 (March 8, 1982): 20–22.

333. Renwick, David. "A Divisive Initiative? Far from Generating Stability in the Caribbean, the U.S.-Inspired Caribbean Basin Initiative May Be Divisive and Lead to the Weakening of CARICOM [Caribbean Community] Just as It Was About to Become More Cohesive." *Caribbean and West Indies Chronicle* 98 (April/May 1982): 10–11.

334. Romero-Barceló, Carlos. "Governor Speaks in Washington on Caribbean Basin Initiative and New Federalism [Particularly as They Affect Puerto Rico]." *Puerto Rico Business Review* 7 (May 1982): 10–18.

335. "Secretary Attends Caribbean Development Meeting [Joint Communique, July 11, and Excerpts from a Conference Held by Secretary of State Haig and U.S. Trade Representative William E. Brock, July 12, 1981]." *Department of State Bulletin* 81 (September 1981): 68–69.

336. Segner, S. F. "The Caribbean Basin: Wait till Next Year?" *Industry Week* 216 (March 21, 1983): 13.

337. Stokes, Bruce. "Reagan's Caribbean Basin Initiative on Track, but Success Still in Doubt." *National Journal* 17 (January 26, 1985): 206–10.

338. "Summary of the Caribbean Basin Initiative (CBI)." *Distribution* 81 (October 1982): 67–68.

339. Theriot, L. "U.S. & FCS and the Caribbean Basin Initiative." *Business America* 7 (March 5, 1984): 9–12.

340. United States. House Committee on Agriculture. Subcommittee on Cotton, Rice, and Sugar. *Review of CBI Sugar Provisions: Hearing, March 31, 1982* (97th Congress, 2d Session). Washington, DC: 1982. 62 p.

341. United States. House Committee on Foreign Affairs. *The Caribbean Basin Initiative: Hearings and Markup, March 23–July 15, 1982, before the Subcommittee on International Economic Policy and Trade and on Inter-American Affairs, "on H.R. 5900"* (97th Congress, 2d Session). Washington, DC: 1982. 600 p.

342. United States. House Committee on Foreign Affairs. *Eastern Caribbean: Report of a Staff Study Mission to the Dominican Republic, Antigua, Dominica, Barbados and St. Vincent, January 5–19, 1982* (97th Congress, 2d Session). Washington, DC: 1982. 22 p.

343. United States. House Committee on Foreign Affairs. Subcommittee on Inter-American Affairs. *Review of Revised Fiscal Year 1982 Economic Assistance Proposals for Latin America and the Caribbean: Hearing, December 15, 1981* (97th Congress, 1st Session). Washington, DC: 1982. 30 p.

344. United States. House Committee on Ways and Means. Subcommittee on Trade. *Caribbean Basin Initiative: Hearings, March 17–25, 1982, on the Administration's Proposed Trade and Tax Measures Affecting the Caribbean Basin* (97th Congress, 2d Session). Washington, DC: 1982. 555 p.

345. United States. Senate Committee on Energy and Natural Resources. *Caribbean Basin Initiative: Hearing, June 10, 1983, on the Caribbean Basin Initiative and Its Relations to the United States Territories and Insular Areas* (98th Congress, 1st Session). Washington, DC: 1983. 110 p.

346. United States. Senate Committee on Finance. *Caribbean Basin Initiative: Hearing, August 2, 1982, on S. 2237* (97th Congress, 2d Session). Washington, DC: 1982. 521 p.

347. United States. Senate Committee on Finance. *Caribbean Basin Initiative, 1983: Hearing, April 13, 1983, on S. 544* (98th Congress, 1st Session). Washington, DC: 1983. 508 p.

348. "U.S. and Israel Assist Caribbean Development." *Business America* 8 (April 29, 1985): 24.

349. Weintraub, Sidney. "U.S. Foreign Economic Policy and Illegal Immigration [Whether the Caribbean Basin Initiative Will Curtail Illegal Immigration from Nearby Countries]." *Population Research and Policy Review* 2 (October 1983): 211–31.

350. Whittle, Richard. "Caribbean Plan Faces Struggle in Congress [President Reagan's Proposed Caribbean Basin Initiative of Aid, Trade Concessions and Tax Incentives]." *Congressional Quarterly Weekly Report* 40 (February 27, 1982): 484–85.

351. Whittle, Richard. "Reagan Wins First Success on Caribbean Plan: Aid Portion Advances [Approval of $350 Million in Economic Aid by the Foreign Affairs Committee, U.S. House of Representatives]." *Congressional Quarterly Weekly Report* 40 (July 24, 1982): 1770–71.

352. "Whittling Away at the Caribbean Initiative [Caribbean Basin Initiative]." *Business Week* (July 11, 1983): 28–29.

353. Wilber, Vincent P. "The Caribbean Basin Initiative: A Plan That Won't Work." *Multinational Monitor* 4 (March 1983): 12–13.

354. Wylie, S. "CBI: One Year Later [Caribbean Basin Initiative]." *Business America* 8 (January 7, 1985): 2–5.

Central America

355. Adams, Dale W. "Foreign Assistance, Economic Policies, and Agriculture in Central America [United States Aid]." *Inter-American Economic Affairs* 38 (Autumn 1984): 45–60.

356. Bolin, William H. "Central America: Real Economic Help Is Workable Now." *Foreign Affairs* 62 (Summer 1984): 1096–1106.

357. Felton, John. "Foreign Aid Bills Facing an Uncertain Future: Central America Is Sticking Point." *Congressional Quarterly Weekly Report* 42 (April 28, 1984): 958–66.

358. Felton, John. "Foreign Aid Controversy: Carter Plan Linking U.S. to Change in Central America Meets Resistance in Congress." *Congressional Quarterly Weekly Report* 38 (April 19, 1980): 1043–46.

359. Felton, John. "On Central America Aid, The Bargaining Begins [President Reagan's Proposal for Development, Economic, and Military Aid in Fiscal Years 1984 and 1985]." *Congressional Quarterly Weekly Report* 42 (February 25, 1984): 443–47.

360. Harrison, Lawrence E. "U.S. Economic Aid Policy in Central America." *Fletcher Forum* 8 (Winter 1984): 33–44.

361. United States. House Committee on Foreign Affairs. Subcommittee on Western Hemisphere Affairs. *Central America: The Ends and Means of U.S. Policy: Hearing, May 2, 1984* (98th Congress, 2d Session). Washington, DC: 1984. 63 p.

362. United States. Senate Committee on Foreign Relations. *National Bipartisan Report on Central America; Hearings, February 7–8, 1984* (98th Congress, 2d Session). Washington, DC: 1984. 432 p.

363. "Who Are We Helping? A Look at U.S. Aid to Central America." *Dollars and Sense* (February 1984): 16–17.

El Salvador

364. Brevetti, Vincent. "U.S. Aid, IMF Loans, and U.S. Companies: Gluing the Salvadoran Economy Together." *Multinational Monitor* 4 (May 1983): 4–5.

365. Madison, Christopher. "Stage for Central America Drama Shifts to the Halls of Congress: The Reagan Administration's Policies in That Troubled Area Are Being Challenged in Congress, and an Early Test Will Come on the Request for More Funds for El Salvador." *National Journal* 15 (April 9, 1983): 740–44.

366. Whittle, Richard. "Senate Panel Would Freeze Foreign Aid for El Salvador [U.S. Senate Foreign Relations Committee Vote to Ban Cash Grants and Military Aid until the Fate of Its Land Reform Program Becomes Clear; Action on Assistance Programs to Several Other Nations]." *Congressional Quarterly Weekly Report* 40 (May 29, 1982): 1255–57.

Guatemala

367. Brockett, Charles D. "The Right to Food and United States Policy in Guatemala [Since World War II]." *Human Rights Quarterly* 6 (August 1984): 366–80.

368. Felton, John. "Congress and Administration Block U.S. Aid to Guatemala: Human Rights Record Scored [Continues Policy in Effect since 1977 of Giving No Military or Economic Aid That Might Imply Active Support for the Government]." *Congressional Quarterly Weekly Report* 41 (December 10, 1983): 2624.

369. Johnston, Ernest B., Jr. "Development Bank Lending to Guatemala." *Department of State Bulletin* 82 (March 1982): 41–43.

Honduras

370. McCormick, P. R. "Why Uncle Sam Is So Welcome in Honduras." *Business Week* (January 16, 1984): 49.

371. Ortiz-Buonafina, Marta. "The CBI Is Not Enough: The Case of Honduras." *Caribbean Review* 14 (Spring 1985): 20–21+.

Nicaragua

372. Jonas, Susanne. "The New Cold War and the Nicaraguan Revolution: The Case of U.S. 'Aid' to Nicaragua." *Contemporary Marxism* (Summer 1981): 89–100.

Dominican Republic

373. United States. Inter-American Foundation. *The Inter-American Foundation in the Dominican Republic: A Decade of Support for Local Government Organizations.* By Robert W. Mashek and Stephen G. Vetter. Rosslyn, VA: 1983. 118 p.

Netherland Antilles

374. "CBI Will Expand Market as Recovery Begins to Ripple through Economy [Caribbean Basin Initiative]." *Business America* 7 (April 30, 1984): 29–30.

Puerto Rico

375. de Onis, Juan. "Puerto Rico: 'Showcase of Democracy' vs. Caribbean Basin Initiative." *Journal of the Institute for Socioeconomic Studies* 7 (Autumn 1982): 599–69.

376. Walker, Ronald. "Puerto Ricans Fear Further Aid Cuts Could Make It a 'Tropical South Bronx'; Many Also Worry That the Reagan Caribbean Initiative Would Negate Some Trade and Tax Advantages Puerto Rico Derives from Its Status as a U.S. Commonwealth." *National Journal* 14 (July 17, 1982): 1253–56.

Latin America

377. Coy, Edward W. "Latin America: Mounting Pressure of Poverty [Emphasis on United States Aid Programs; Based on His Testimony before the Subcommittee on Inter-American Affairs, Committee on International Relations, U.S. House of Representatives, February 12, 1980]." *Agenda* 3 (April 1980): 16–19.

378. DiGiovanni, Cleto, Jr. *The Inter-American Foundation.* Washington, DC: Heritage Foundation, 1981. 89 p.

379. Gonzalez, Heliodoro. "Can Foreign Aid Continue as a Growth Industry for the Bureaucracy? Latin American Cooperation at the United Nations [Voting Patterns of 20 Latin American Countries during the 36th United Nations General Assembly (1981–82); Whether the United States Should Use Foreign Aid to Influence Voting]." *Inter-American Economic Affairs* 37 (Summer 1983): 53–60.

380. "Latin America Aid Backed." *Engineering News-Record* 212 (January 19, 1984): 13–14.

381. United States. House Committee on Foreign Affairs. Subcommittee on Inter-American Affairs. *Review of Revised Fiscal Year 1982 Economic Assistance Proposals for Latin America and the Caribbean: Hearing, December 15, 1981* (97th Congress, 1st Session). Washington, DC: 1982. 30 p.

Argentina

382. Berg, Gracia. "Human Rights Sanctions as Leverage: Argentina, a Case Study [Whether the Imposition of Such Sanctions by the United States Have Been Effective]." *Journal of Legislation* 7 (1980): 93–112.

Peru

383. "Testing Ground for the Reagan Brand of Foreign Aid." *Business Week* (April 19, 1982): 56+.

COMMERCE AND TRADE

Mexico

384. Anderson, E. V. "North American Trade Alliance Gains Support." *Chemical & Engineering News* 58 (July 14, 1980): 12–14+.

385. Baerresen, Donald W. "The Value of Imports through U.S. Ports on the Mexican Border." *Texas Business Review* 55 (September/October 1981): 192–95.

386. Baldwin, L. "Mexico Toughens Its Auto Trade Rules." *Automotive News* (October 19, 1981): 12.

387. "Boxcars Snarl Mexican Trade." *Business Week* (February 9, 1981): 46.

388. Brown, K. M. "North American Trade Policies: Implications for U.S. Business Firms." *Business Economics* 17 (January 1982): 47–55.

389. Buchanan, R., and Rhein, R., Jr. "A First Step toward Freer Trade with the U.S." *Business Week* (May 6, 1985): 61.

390. "Computers Aid Business for U.S. and Mexican Customs Brokers." *American Import/Export Bulletin* 94 (February 1981): 22.

391. "Congestion Eases at Border." *Railway Age* 182 (July 13, 1981): 14.

392. Crowley, C. B. "U.S. Show Will Take Advantage of Growing Market in Mexico for Pollution Control Equipment." *Business America* 6 (December 12, 1983): 38–39.

393. "Dangerous Precedent in Trade [Chemicals; Editorial]." *Chemical Week* 129 (December 23, 1981): 3.

394. Eckhardt, K. B. "Water Route to Mexico." *American Import/Export Bulletin* 94 (February 1981): 26+.

395. "Economic Growth Likely to Slow to 5 Percent in 1982: Policies of New President May Effect Economy, Market." *Business America* 5 (January 11, 1982): 22–24.

396. Hirschhorn, J. S. "Mexican Steel and American Policy." *Challenge* 23 (January/February 1981): 57–58.

397. "How Carmakers Are Trimming an Import Surplus." *Business Week* (January 30, 1984): 36–37.

398. Hufbauer, Gary Clyde, et al. "Bilateral Trade Relations." *Proceedings of the Academy of Political Science* 34 (1) (1981): 136–45.

399. Huffman, W. E. "International Trade in Labor versus Commodities; U.S.-Mexican Agriculture." *American Journal of Agricultural Economics* 64 (December 1982): 989–98.

400. Major, M. "Mexican Markets: Moving up from Fifth to Third in Two Years to Rival Japan as the Second-Placed U.S. Trade Partner." *American Import/Export Management* 96 (February 1982): 14+.

401. "Mexican Import Licensing Changes Open Market to Many U.S. Goods." *Business America* 8 (November 11, 1985): 16–17.

402. "Mexico: Boom or Bust for U.S. Traders." *American Import/Export Bulletin* 94 (February 1981): 14+.

403. "Mexico: Credit Terms May Hurt a Big U.S. Nuclear Sale." *Business Week* (November 30, 1981): 64.

404. "Mexico: A Major Market for U.S. Products." *Business America* 3 (June 16, 1980): 3–7.

405. "Mexico Seen Subsidizing Exports of Ammonia." *Oil & Gas Journal* 81 (April 11, 1983): 66.

406. "Mexico: Trading across the Border by Rail." *American Import/Export Bulletin* 94 (February 1981): 16+.

407. "Mexico-U.S. Joint Commission on Commerce and Trade Meets in Inaugural Session." *Business America* 4 (October 19, 1981): 15.

408. "Mexico-U.S. Trade Agreement Snags on Drug Patent Issue: Could Affect Ammonia Test." *Chemical Marketing Reporter* 225 (June 25, 1984): 7.

409. "Mexico's Grain Binge: Buy Now, Pay Never?" *Business Week* (June 13, 1983): 35.

410. "New Visa Procedures Facilitate U.S. Business Visits to Mexico." *Business America* 5 (September 6, 1982): 28–29.

411. "No End in Sight for Mexican Rail Embargo." *Handling & Shipping Management* 22 (February 1981): 13.

412. Pendzich, C. "Economy Slows down but Still Has Room for Imports." *Business America* 8 (September 16, 1985): 17–18.

413. "President Reports to Congress on Efforts to Expand U.S. Trade with North American Neighbors." *Business America* 4 (August 24, 1981): 14–15.

414. Presti, S. M. "U.S. Exports Increase as Adjustment Continues." *Business America* 7 (August 20, 1984): 25–26.

415. Presti, S. M., and Bawer, L. G. "Eximbank Sets up Facilities to Spur U.S. Exports to Brazil and Mexico." *Business America* 6 (December 12, 1983): 34–35.

416. Rhein, R., Jr. "A U.S.-Mexico Pact on Trade." *Chemical Week* 136 (April 24, 1985): 18.

417. Rubio Sánchez, Antonio, et al. "Mexican-United States Trade Relations." *Comercio Exterior de Mexico* 27 (March 1981): 118–24; (April 1981): 167–74.

418. Schmitz, A., et al. "Agricultural Export Dumping: The Case of Mexican Winter Vegetables in the U.S. Market." *American Journal of Agricultural Economics* 63 (November 1981): 645–54.

419. "Shippers Hands Aren't Tied by Mexican Standoff." *Distribution* 80 (March 1981): 16.

420. Taylor, T. J. "Economy Improves, Offers Opportunities for Business." *Business America* 8 (March 4, 1985): 38–39.

421. Tower, F. J. "Changed Conditions Face U.S. Exporters to Mexico." *Business America* 5 (October 4, 1982): 21.

422. Tower, F. J. "Economic Retrenchment Brings U.S. Exports Down." *Business America* 6 (August 22, 1983): 7–8.

423. Tower, F. J. "Economy Is Adjusting after Peso Devaluation." *Business America* 5 (August 9, 1982): 47–48.

424. Tower, F. J. "New Administration Cites Progress, Charts Recovery." *Business America* 7 (February 20, 1984): 26.

425. Tower, F. J. "Selling Is More Difficult in This Changing Economy." *Business America* 5 (February 8, 1982): 17–18.

426. Tower, F. J. "Upsurge in Trade Makes This Third-Ranking U.S. Market." *Business America* 4 (February 9, 1981): 48.

427. Tower, F. J. "U.S. Suppliers Can Expect Tougher Stance on Imports." *Business America* 4 (July 27, 1981): 22–23.

428. "Trade with the United States Is Increasing as Economy Rebounds; Subsidies Agreement Improves Relationship." *Business America* 8 (June 24, 1985): 25–26.

429. Truett, Dale B., and Truett, Lila Florey. "Mexico and GSP: Problems and Prospects [Experience with United States Generalized System of Preferences]." *Inter-American Economic Affairs* 34 (Autumn 1980): 67–85.

430. Turner, R. "Practical Advice on Exporting to Mexico." *Business America* 5 (November 15, 1982): 18–22.

431. "U.S. Ammonia Makers Balk over Subsidies [Mexico's Feedstock Subsidies to Build up Export Industries]." *Chemical Week* 131 (November 10, 1982): 38.

432. "U.S. Chemical Makers Seek Import Duties on Subsidized Goods." *Chemical Marketing Reporter* 222 (July 26, 1982) 3+.

433. Weiner, B. "Mexican Markets in '83: A Toss up for U.S. Traders!" *American Import-Export Management* 98 (February 1983): 22–23.

434. "Will the U.S. Preempt Private Grain Sales?" *Business Week* (June 16, 1980): 67+.

435. Zubryn, E. "Mexico Moves to Ban Certain Cosmetic Imports." *Drug & Cosmetic Industry* 136 (February 1985): 35+.

436. Zubryn, E. "Mexico's Import Lid to Hurt, Then Help." *Automotive News* (January 11, 1982): 26.

Central America

437. Bastian, W. "Despite Political Unrest, Area Offers Opportunities." *Business America* 2 (July 30, 1979): 8.

438. Borakove, M. "Caribbean Basin Recovery Act [Duty-Free Treatment for the Caribbean and Central American Region]." *American Import/Export Management* 99 (November 1983): 70.

439. "Cutting Capital's Strings: An Interview with Michael Manley." *Multinational Monitor* 6 (May 1985): 4–6.

440. "Dilemmas of Caribbean Development: An Overview with G. Arthur Brown." *Fletcher Forum* 9 (Summer 1985): 255–68.

441. Knee, R. "Central America Trade Is Suddenly Crowded." *American Shipper* 27 (March 1985): 64.

442. Turner, Harry L. "Caribbean Basin Initiative: Promising after Its First Year." *Caribbean Today* 2 (May 1985): 23–27.

443. Vega, Bernardo. "The CBI Faces Adversity: Lessons from the Asian Export Strategy." *Caribbean Review* 14 (Spring 1985): 18–19+.

444. Watson, Hilbourne A. "The Caribbean Basin Initiative and Caribbean Development: A Critical Analysis." *Contemporary Marxism* (10) (1985): 1–37.

Costa Rica

445. "Adverse Economic Trends Are Continuing in 1982; But There Is Still Opportunity for Some U.S. Firms." *Business America* 5 (May 3, 1982): 31–32.

446. "Export Growth Should Generate Adequate Foreign Exchange to Increase Imports and Stimulate the Economy by 1984." *Business America* 6 (June 27, 1983): 22–23.

El Salvador

447. "Economic Decline Ends: Prospects Are Good for Selected U.S. Products." *Business America* 7 (November 12, 1984): 35–37.

448. McQueen, C. "U.S. Traders and Investors Will Find a Strong Market." *Business America* 7 (August 20, 1984): 50.

449. "Patient Exporters Could Find This a Lucrative Market after Economic and Political Difficulties Are Overcome." *Business America* 6 (May 2, 1983): 28–29.

450. "Trade Fair Reveals Good Prospects for U.S. in El Salvador." *Business America* 5 (November 29, 1982): 33.

Guatemala

451. "Success in Containing the Guerrilla Insurgency Will Help Determine the Strength and Timing of Economic Recovery." *Business America* 6 (April 18, 1983): 26–28.

Honduras

452. "Country's Limited Foreign Exchange Stems Growth of Needed American Imports." *Business America* 8 (August 19, 1985): 19–20.
453. Pugh, D. C. "Small but Growing Market Close to U.S. Has Money to Spend for Imports." *Business America* 3 (September 8, 1980): 25–26.

Nicaragua

454. "Economic Performance Is Projected to Remain Dismal." *Business America* 8 (April 1, 1985): 27–28.
455. Heard, J., and Kruckewitt, J., "How Washington's Allies Are Aiding the Sandinistas [Reaction to U.S. Embargo]." *Business Week* (July 29, 1985): 45.
456. "More of a Tickle Than a Bodyblow." *Economist* 295 (May 4, 1985): 28.
457. "Nixing Trade with Nicaragua." *Fortune* 111 (May 27, 1985): 8.
458. Pearson, J., et al. "Is Reagan's Target Managua or Congress? [Embargo against Nicaragua]." *Business Week* (May 13, 1985): 45.
459. "Uncertain Economy and Sales Characteristics Offer Challenge, Opportunity." *Business America* 4 (October 19, 1981): 21.

Panama

460. "Economy Still Suffers Effects of Worldwide Recession but Attractive Opportunities Remain for U.S. Business." *Business America* 6 (September 19, 1983): 21–23.
461. Holcomb, S. "Panama's Growth Highlights Market Developments Here." *Business America* 4 (July 27, 1981): 24.
462. Kolbenschlag, M. "Going for Profits Uncle Sam Ignored." *Forbes* 125 (March 17, 1980): 91+.

Caribbean Basin

463. "Caribbean Basin Initiative Should Help Bolster Export Industries and Reverse Long Slide into Recession." *Business America* 7 (May 14, 1984): 32–34.

Dominican Republic

464. "Country Continues to Offer Good Opportunities for U.S. Trade and Investment Despite Its Serious Economic Woes." *Business America* 7 (October 15, 1984): 33–35.

465. "Downturn in the Economy Affects Market Prospects." *Business America* 5 (January 25, 1982): 25–26.

466. Fermoselle, R. "FCS Officials in Santo Domingo Get out from behind the Desk to Help Market American Goods." *Business America* 5 (August 23, 1982): 10–11.

467. Fermoselle, R. "U.S. Commerce Department and Florida Coordinate Export Development Activities." *Business America* 6 (April 4, 1983): 12–13.

468. "Major Construction Projects Offer Some of Most Promising Trade and Investment Opportunities for American Business." *Business America* 4 (April 20, 1981): 23–24.

Latin America

469. Anderson, E. V. "Chemical Trade Balance Vexes Latin Firms." *Chemical & Engineering News* 61 (December 12, 1983): 13.

470. "Aviation Services Firms Explore Opportunities in Latin America." *Business America* 8 (July 22, 1985): 16–17.

471. Behrman, Jere R. "Exports of Non-Fuel Primary Products [Latin America: Conference Paper]." *CEPAL Review* (April 1980): 32–48.

472. Brewer, T. K. "Latin America Markets Expand with Mexico Leading the Way." *Business America* 2 (July 30, 1979): 5.

473. Brewer, T. K. "Seven Latin American Nations Offer Billion-Dollar Markets." *Business America* 3 (February 11, 1980): 44–45.

474. Brewer, T. K. "Sustained Growth Projected in Key Latin American Markets." *Business America* 4 (February 9, 1981): 47.

475. Brewer, T. K. "U.S. Exporters Face Slower Economies in Latin America." *Business America* 4 (July 27, 1981): 21.

476. Brewer, T. K. "U.S. Exports to Latin America Should Top $30 Billion in 1980." *Business America* 3 (July 28, 1980): 50.

477. "A Buoyant Market for U.S. Exports." *Latin American Times* 2 (February 1980): 12+.

478. Cavan, B. "Trade Is up in Latin America, U.S. Exports Making Comeback." *Business America* 7 (August 20, 1984): 24–25.

479. Conger, S. M. "U.S. Exports to Latin America to Hold Firm as Markets Slow." *Business America* 5 (February 8, 1982): 16–17.

480. Dhar, S. "U.S. Trade with Latin America: Consequences of Financing Constraints." *Federal Reserve Bank of New York Quarterly Review* 8 (Autumn 1983): 14–18.

481. Dooley, B. J. "Latin Markets." *American Import/Export Management* 96 (January 1982): 20.

482. Edwards, R. S. "U.S. Apparel Exporters Go South, Explore Growing Latin Markets." *Business America* 5 (January 11, 1982): 12–13.

483. "Foreign Fishing Policies of Latin American Nations." *Marine Fisheries Review* 43 (February 1981): 27–29.

484. Frundt, H. "Fat Latin Profits for U.S. Agribusiness." *Business and Society Review* (34) (Summer 1980): 15–20.

485. Griffiths, D. R. "Latin Sales Hinge on Stability, Sanctions." *Aviation Week & Space Technology* 110 (June 11, 1979): 307+.

486. Kane, B. "Exports to Latin America Booming." *Automotive News* (September 15, 1980): 15.

487. Keenan, R. "Growing Demand for Diverse Products Open New Export Markets in South America." *Management Review* 68 (October 1979): 47.

488. Kolcum, E. H. "Latin American Market Draws New Competitors." *Aviation Week & Space Technology* 114 (February 23, 1981): 49–50.

489. Kolcum, E. H. "Latin Aviation Needs Offer Challenge to U.S. Industry." *Aviation Week & Space Technology* 116 (June 21, 1982): 35–36.

490. Kolcum, E. H. "U.S. Seeks Larger Latin Airport Market." *Aviation Week & Space Technology* 120 (June 18, 1984): 40–41+.

491. "Latin America Focuses on Debt, Balance-of-Payments Problems." *Business America* 7 (February 20, 1984): 25–26.

492. Lofgren, J. G. "U.S. Exporters to Latin America Face Difficult Challenges in 1983." *Business America* 6 (February 21, 1983): 46–47.

493. "Management Q & A: Dealing with Latin America." *Management Review* 74 (February 1985): 15.

494. Muller, E. J. "Tierra de Promeso, Tierra de Miero [Land of Promise and Fear]." *Distribution* 84 (October 1985): 11+.

495. Mye, R. "U.S. Exporters to Latin America Face Difficult Markets in 1982." *Business America* 5 (August 9, 1982): 46–47.

496. Odell, John S. "Latin American Trade Negotiations with the United States [Bilateral Bargaining to Regulate Trade and Market Shares: Some of the Techniques Used to Settle Such Disputes]." *International Organization* 34 (Spring 1980): 207–28.

497. Oppenheimer, A. "Florida Ports See '84 Surge in Latin Imports." *American Import/Export Management* 99 (November 1983): 66–67+.

498. "Pan American Day Review—1981 [Trade and Business Trends in the Americas]." *Journal of Commerce and Commercial* 348 (April 13, 1981): 1A–6A.

499. Pinto, Anibal. "The Opening up of Latin America to the Exterior." *CEPAL Review* (August 1980): 31–56.

500. "President Discusses Trade Policy with Latin American Leaders." *Business America* 5 (December 27, 1982): 20.

501. "Raid on U.S. Tuna Rights." *Business Week* (May 14, 1979): 58–59.

502. Rice, R. "Foreign Debt Problem Clouds Latin America Trade Outlook." *Business America* 6 (August 22, 1983): 6–7.

503. Roth, R. F. "There's More Gold in Enchiladas Than in Fortune Cookies." *Industrial Marketing* 64 (November 1979): 76–77.

504. Straus, D. B. "Why International Commercial Arbitration Is Lagging in Latin America: Problems and Cures." *Arbitration Journal* 33 (March 1978): 21–24.

505. Taylor, T. J. "Latin America Outlook Improves as Adjustment Efforts Continue." *Business America* 8 (March 4, 1985): 37–38.

506. "Trade Mission to South America Finds Keen Interest in U.S. Fire, Security and Safety Equipment." *Business America* 7 (May 28, 1984): 41.

507. "U.S. Skids to Fourth Position in Latin American Arms Sales." *Aviation Week & Space Technology* 110 (March 5, 1979): 46.

Argentina

508. Hage, W. "Argentina: Expansion of U.S. Exports Follows Trade Liberalization." *Business America* 3 (February 11, 1980): 45.

509. Hynes, K. "U.S. Export Shipments Will Reach $1 Billion." *Business America* 2 (July 30, 1979): 7.

510. Kelly, G. L. "New President Aims to Continue Open Import Policy in Fourth Largest U.S. Market in Latin America." *Business America* 4 (June 1, 1981): 27–29.

Bolivia

511. Beargie, T. "Cargo Pact for Land-Locked Bolivia [Linabol and Lykes Bros.]." *American Shipper* 25 (April 1983): 42.

Brazil

512. Ahern, E. "Dull Economy Dampens Growth of U.S. Exports." *Business America* 5 (August 9, 1982): 49.

513. Anderson, E. V. "Battle Rages over Imports of Fuel Ethanol." *Chemical & Engineering News* 63 (April 22, 1985): 9–15.

514. Bawer, L. G. "Austerity Program Limits Import Market." *Business America* 6 (August 22, 1983): 8–9.

515. Bawer, L. G. "Foreign Debt Constrains U.S. Export Opportunities." *Business America* 6 (February 21, 1983): 48.

516. Beargie, T. "American Atlantic and Brazilian Officials Told by FMC They Have until Oct. 5 to Work out a Cargo Pooling Arrangement." *American Shipper* 24 (September 1982): 92.

517. "Brazil Hangs Tough on Market Protection." *International Management* 40 (November 1985): 7.

518. "Brazil: How Shivering Florida Is Warming a Rival." *Business Week* (February 1, 1982): 39.

519. "Brazil Proposes Aircraft Import Tariff Cuts, Automatic Licensing." *Aviation Week & Space Technology* 124 (February 3, 1986): 61.

520. "Brazil: Trade Troubles Strain Relations with the U.S." *Business Week* (September 13, 1982): 47.

521. "Brazilian Export Policy Sparks Criticism." *Aviation Week & Space Technology* 116 (June 21, 1982): 60–61.

522. "Business Regroups in Wake of Rare Recession; Restrictive Import Policies Limit Market Potential." *Business America* 5 (May 3, 1982): 24–25.

523. "The Current Economic Crisis Limits Market Potential, but New Exim Facility Will Help U.S. Firms Compete." *Business America* 7 (July 9, 1984): 30–32.

524. "Drought, Floods, Oil Prices Affect Trade Picture, Dash Hopes for Liberalization of Import Policy." *Business America* 2 (November 5, 1979): 22–23.

525. Earle, W. "Improved Economy Creates New Export Opportunities." *Business America* 7 (August 20, 1984): 27+.

526. Earle, W. "1985 Is an Opportune Time to Look at This Market." *Business America* 8 (March 4, 1985): 40.

527. "Economic Readjustment Policy Should Brighten Future but Recession and Restrictions Limit Present Market." *Business America* 6 (July 11, 1983): 20–21.

528. "Eximbank Readies Credit Facility for Exports to Brazil." *Business America* 7 (June 11, 1984): 25.

529. "Fairchild Appeals ITC's Denial of Bandeirante Import Duties." *Aviation Week & Space Technology* 117 (November 22, 1982): 64–65.

530. "Frost That Saved Brazil's Orange Trade." *Business Week* (February 9, 1981): 25+.

531. Garges, L. "Continuing Recession Limits Import Market." *Business America* 7 (February 20, 1984): 27–28.

532. Garges, L. "Tight Import Market Keeps U.S. Sales in Holding Pattern." *Business America* 2 (July 30, 1979): 6–7.

533. Garges, L. "U.S. Exports down in '81, Seen Rebounding This Year." *Business America* 5 (February 8, 1982): 18.

534. Garges, L. "U.S. Products Perform Well in Tightened Import Market." *Business America* 4 (July 27, 1981): 22.

535. "Government Brakes Economy with Tight Money Policies: U.S. Sales Grow but Import Restrictions Limit Potential." *Business America* 4 (November 16, 1981): 17–18.

536. "Government Tries to Stem Tide of Economic Decline." *Business America* 7 (September 17, 1984): 28.

537. Hughes, A. H. "Fiske Visit Opens New Era of Commercial Relations with Brazil." *Business America* 6 (May 2, 1983): 2–6.

538. Johnson, T. "U.S./Brazil Accords Are Leading toward Commercial Contracts for Energy Projects." *Business America* 6 (October 3, 1983): 15–16.

539. Levinson, Marc. "Trade and Jobs: The Brazilian Connection; The Foreign Debt Hits Home [Brazilian Export Program to Pay Interest on the Country's Debts; Effect on the Manufacturing Sector in the United States]." *Worldview* 27 (December 1984): 9–11.

540. Levinson, Marc. "What to Do about Brazil Inc. [Redefining Relationship with U.S.]." *Across the Board* 22 (March 1985): 40–46.

541. McCown, H. "New U.S.-Brazilian Accords Explained to Business at Commerce Seminar." *Business America* 6 (June 13, 1983): 24–25.

542. Miller, H. G. "Three Months Left to Change Bilateral Policy." *American Shipper* 27 (October 1985): 10+.

543. Neale, T. "Another U.S.-Flag Failure [American Atlantic Service to Brazil]." *American Shipper* 25 (April 1983): 58.

544. "Normalized Relations with Principal Trading Partners Could Facilitate Recovery." *Business America* 5 (March 8, 1982): 30–31.

545. North, D. M. "Import Duties on Bandeirante Weighed." *Aviation Week & Space Technology* 117 (September 20, 1982): 115.

546. Pinckney, K. "Brazilian Trading Firm Stumbles; Recoups [Brazil-America Commodities Corp.]." *American Shipper* 26 (December 1984): 74+.

547. Pinkow, E. S. "Brazil: New Economic Reforms Limit Prospects for Trade Growth." *Business America* 3 (February 11, 1980): 48–49.

548. Presti, S. M., and Bawer, L. G. "Eximbank Sets up Facilities to Spur U.S. Exports to Brazil and Mexico." *Business America* 6 (December 12, 1983): 34–35.

549. Sarathy, R. "High-Technology Exports from Newly Industrializing Countries: The Brazilian Commuter Aircraft Industry." *California Management Review* 27 (Winter 1985): 60–84.

550. "Signs of Economic Recovery Point to Increased Prospects for American Investments and Exports in Selected Sectors." *Business America* 8 (July 22, 1985): 22–23.

551. "The Trade Deal May Be Just Hot Air." *Business Week* (May 2, 1983): 43.

552. Welsh, E. "Cash in on FINEX Financing [Fundo de Financiamento a Exportacao]." *American Import/Export Management* 101 (December 1984): 47.

553. "Whose Facts Are to Be Trusted? [Claims That Bilateral Shipping Agreements Bring on Higher Shipping Rates]." *American Shipper* 25 (September 1983): 37–38.

Chile

554. "Chile Fishing License Regulations Outlined." *Marine Fisheries Review* 42 (May 1980): 38–39.

555. "Five-Year Boom Is over until at Least Mid-1982: New Trade Financing Measures May Cut into U.S. Exports." *Business America* 5 (March 8, 1982): 28–29.

556. Lacey, D. C., Jr. "Economic Performance Remains Strong on All Fronts: Free Trade Policy Creates Buoyant Import Market." *Business America* 2 (October 22, 1979): 18+.

557. Lindow, Herbert. "Chile: Healthy Economic Growth Boosts Import Demand." *Business America* 3 (February 11, 1980): 49.

558. Lindow, Herbert. "Doors Are Open to Imports in This Competitive Market." *Business America* 4 (July 27, 1981): 26.

559. Lindow, Herbert. "Financial Problems, World Conditions Cloud Forecast." *Business America* 6 (February 21, 1983): 48–49.

560. Lindow, Herbert. "Import Demand Declines during Economic Lull." *Business America* 5 (August 9, 1982): 50.

561. Lindow, Herbert. "Imports to Rise Modestly as Recovery Continues." *Business America* 8 (March 4, 1985): 41.

562. Lindow, Herbert. "Market Unlikely to Grow as Economy Slows in '82." *Business America* 5 (February 8, 1982): 21.

563. Lindow, Herbert. "Moderate Growth Expected after Severe Recession." *Business America* 7 (February 20, 1984): 28.

564. Lindow, Herbert. "Recovery Brings Moderate Rebound for U.S. Exports." *Business America* 7 (August 20, 1984): 32.

565. Lindow, Herbert. "Slow Recovery Portends Slight Rise in U.S. Sales." *Business America* 6 (August 22, 1983): 12.

566. "New Financial Package Eases Debt Burden with Banks: U.S. Suppliers Continue to Face Keen Competition." *Business America* 8 (September 2, 1985): 16–17.

567. "Open-to-Import Market Has Good U.S. Export Prospects." *Business America* 8 (June 10, 1985): 21–22.

568. "Projected 4–5 Percent Rise in Gross National Product Could Result in Significant Increase in Imports in '84." *Business America* 7 (June 25, 1984): 29–31.

569. "Recession Has a Firm Grip on the Economy; Efforts to Cope with Debt Problem Make Importers Wary." *Business America* 6 (May 30, 1983): 24–26.

Colombia

570. "Colombia: Economic Growth Rate Continues to Accelerate: Outlook Is Excellent for U.S. Sales During 1979." *Business America* 2 (May 7, 1979): 16–17.

571. "Limited Foreign Exchange and Slow Economic Growth Could Repress 1986 Sales." *Business America* 8 (November 11, 1985): 25–27.

572. Muenzer, R. F. "Colombia: Infrastructure Developments Boost U.S. Sales, Investment." *Business America* 3 (February 11, 1980): 47–48.

573. Muenzer, R. F. "More Foreign Exchange Is Available for Imports." *Business America* 5 (February 8, 1982): 19.

574. Muenzer, R. F. "New Development Plan Aids Economic Prospects." *Business America* 7 (February 20, 1984): 29.

575. Muenzer, R. F. "Restrictive Market Still Depresses Import Levels." *Business America* 8 (March 4, 1985): 42.

576. Muenzer, R. F. "Tight Import Restraints Retard Economic Recovery." *Business America* 7 (August 20, 1984): 31.

577. Muenzer, R. F. "U.S. Sales Hold Firm in Weaker Import Market." *Business America* 4 (July 27, 1981): 23.

578. Ponsar, D. "Exports, Reserves Drop as Economy Declines." *Business America* 6 (August 22, 1983): 10–11.

579. "Still Counting on Coffee." *Euromoney* (September 1983 supp): 18–21.

580. "Timing of Economic Recovery Depends on Effectiveness of New Administration's Program and Foreign Demand." *Business America* 5 (October 4, 1982): 22–23.

Ecuador

581. "Economy Still Winding down from Petroleum Boom: Market Is Good for a Wide Range of U.S. Products." *Business America* 4 (November 2, 1981): 24–26.

582. "Government Moves to Put Economic House in Order." *Business America* 6 (October 31, 1983): 31–33.

583. "Imports Are Liberalized, but Foreign Exchange Shortage Still Limits Import Growth." *Business America* 8 (October 28, 1985): 19–21.

584. Lindow, Herbert. "U.S. Exports Benefiting from Oil-Based Prosperity." *Business America* 2 (July 30, 1979): 9.

585. "Public Sector Spending Keeps Growth Rate Respectable and Sustains Demand for U.S. Products and Services." *Business America* 5 (April 5, 1982): 27–29.

586. "Several Factors Dampen Economic Growth Prospects, but This Remains a Major Market for U.S. Exports." *Business America* 5 (September 20, 1982): 24–27.

Paraguay

587. "Complex Business Climate Requires Exporters to Be Cautious but Persistent." *Business America* 7 (October 15, 1984): 35–37.

588. "Recession Replaces Boom, but Economy Still Offers a Range of Opportunities." *Business America* 5 (July 12, 1982): 28–29.

589. "U.S. Firms Need to Sell Their Products More Aggressively to Meet the Growing Competition from Other Countries." *Business America* 6 (July 25, 1983): 22–23.

Peru

590. Keenan, R. "Growing Demand for Diverse Products Opens New Export Markets in South America." *Management Review* 68 (October 1979): 47.

591. Lindow, Herbert. "Favorable Terms of Trade Buoy U.S. Export Prospects." *Business America* 6 (February 21, 1983): 52.

592. Lindow, Herbert. "International Debt Difficulties Auger Lower Import Level." *Business America* 8 (March 4, 1985): 42–43.

593. Lindow, Herbert. "Lower U.S. Export Levels Are Anticipated in 1982." *Business America* 5 (August 9, 1982): 51.

594. Lindow, Herbert. "Market-Oriented Economy Opens Sales Opportunities." *Business America* 4 (February 9, 1981): 49.

595. Lindow, Herbert. "Recession, Austerity to Continue into 1984." *Business America* 7 (February 20, 1984): 30.

596. Lindow, Herbert. "Recession Puts Damper on Demand for Imports." *Business America* 7 (August 20, 1984): 32.

597. Lindow, Herbert. "Trade Liberalizationn Brings Import Surge." *Business America* 4 (July 27, 1981): 26.

598. Lindow, Herbert. "U.S. Exports Drop Further, Likely to Rebound in 1984." *Business America* 6 (August 22, 1983): 12.

599. Lindow, Herbert. "U.S. Sales Likely to Grow at Slower Pace in 1982." *Business America* 5 (February 8, 1982): 21.

600. Nelton, S. "Their Woolgathering Is No Daydream [Peruvian Connection]." *Nation's Business* 73 (July 1985): 36.

601. "Stymied Trade Talks Keep Peru's President at Home." *Business Week* (November 22, 1982): 55.

602. Wentz, L. "Peru's Market Boom Shaky but Media Are Busting Out." *Advertising Age* 53 (sec 2) (July 5, 1982): M22.

Uruguay

603. "Economy Is Slowed by Impact of the World Recession, Challenged by the Need for Major Structural Changes." *Business America* 5 (August 23, 1982): 18–19.

604. "Economy Slowed by Impact of World Recession; American Exporters Will Find Market Challenging." *Business America* 6 (July 11, 1983): 22–24.

Venezuela

605. Banks, S. M. "Rebound in Oil Market Needed to Spark Economy." *Business America* 5 (August 9, 1982): 51–52.

606. Beargie, T. "CCT Seems Satisfied, but Problems with Venezuela Trade Still Linger." *American Shipper* 25 (April 1983): 77.

607. Beargie, T. "Faced with FMC Action, Venezuela Reopens Trade." *American Shipper* 25 (March 1983): 11.

608. Beargie, T. "FMC Pressures Venezuela with Sec. 19 Warning; Could Impose Tariff Suspension or Service Restriction Effective Jan. 15." *American Shipper* 25 (January 1983): 47.

609. Beargie, T. "Squeezed Out? CCT Was No. 1 in Venezuelan Trade Last May; Has Dropped to No. 4 and Wants Help from FMC." *American Shipper* 24 (December 1982): 14+.

610. Beargie, T. "U.S. & Venezuela Views Far Apart." *American Shipper* 25 (July 1983): 6.

611. "Combination of Factors Expected to Boost Demand in Venezuela for U.S. Construction Equipment." *Business America* 4 (November 16, 1981): 14–15.

612. "Concorde/Nopal Expects to Maintain Third-Flag Share in Venezuelan Market." *American Shipper* 25 (May 1983): 63.

613. Earle, W. "Economy Sputters but Oil Income Pays for Imports." *Business America* 5 (February 8, 1982): 20–21.

614. "Healthcare Market in Venezuela." *Business America* 4 (September 7, 1981): 14–15.

615. Jacka, T. R. "Emphasis on Social Services Creates New Export Market." *Business America* 2 (July 30, 1979): 9.

616. Jacka, T. R. "Venezuela: Second Largest Latin Market for U.S. Combats Imbalance." *Business America* 3 (February 11, 1980): 47.

617. Miles, K. "Market Growth Should Continue at a Slow Pace." *Business America* 8 (March 4, 1985): 41–42.

618. Montoulieu, C. F. "Adjustment Measures Curb Imports, Delay Payments." *American Shipper* 6 (August 22, 1983): 11.

619. Montoulieu, C. F. "Economic Problems Continue but Trade Makes Recovery." *Business America* 7 (August 20, 1984): 30.

620. Montoulieu, C. F. "New Administration Faces Bad Economic Recession." *Business America* 7 (February 20, 1984): 29–30.

621. Montoulieu, C. F. "Stagnating Economy Limits Prospects for U.S. Exports." *Business America* 6 (February 21, 1983): 50.

622. "Shipper Voice in Cargo Policy Negotiations [Frank L. Merwin]." *American Shipper* 25 (July 1983): 3–4.

623. "Venezuela." *American Import/Export Management* 96 (January 1982): 21.

624. "Why Should We Buy from You If We Can't Sell to You?" *Forbes* 135 (June 3, 1985): 48+.

ECONOMIC DEVELOPMENT

Nicaragua

625. Adkins, Jason. "Taking Care of Business in Nicaragua." *Multinational Monitor* 5 (April 1985): 3–15.

626. Roberts, Charles. "Nicaragua: The Unfolding Scene [Possible Effects of Current Government Economic Policies on United States Corporate Investments in Nicaragua]." *Multinational Monitor* 1 (March 1980): 18–20.

Panama

627. "Officials Evaluate Investment Climate, Business Opportunities in Panama." *Business America* 2 (September 10, 1979): 11.

Latin America

628. Galbis, V. "Money, Investment, and Growth in Latin America, 1961–1973." *Economic Development and Cultural Change* 27 (April 1979): 423–43.

629. Holden, K., and Peel, D. A. "Relationship between Prices and Money Supply in Latin America, 1958–1975." *Review of Economics and Statistics* 61 (August 1979): 446–50.

630. "Latin America: Only the Oil Exporters Escape Wild Inflation." *Business Week* (October 22, 1979): 95–96.

631. "Latin America: Region of Economic Contradiction. [Special Report]." *Euromoney Supp* (April 1980): i–xxiv.

632. Shaw, T. M. "Semiperiphery in Africa and Latin America: Subimperialism and Semiindustrialism." *Review of Black Political Economy* 9 (Summer 1979): 341–58.

Argentina

633. Bastian, W. "Administration's Economic Policies Will Be Tested." *Business America* 5 (August 9, 1982): 48.

634. Bastian, W. "Economy Is in Transition; Market Remains Sluggish." *Business America* 6 (August 22, 1983): 10.

635. Bastian, W. "Wide Range of Ills Make This a Year of Transition." *Business America* 6 (February 21, 1983): 47.

636. Beargie, T. "How the Squeeze Was Put on Ivaran [Ivaran Lines]." *American Shipper* 26 (November 1984): 12+.

637. "The Economic Effects of the Argentine Crisis." *United States Banker* 93 (September 1982): 38.

638. Fondevilla, R. E. "Under-Exploited South Atlantic Whiting Frozen in Argentina for U.S. Market." *Quick Frozen Foods* 41 (May 1979): 82.

639. "Hyperinflation Kicks off a Spending Binge." *Business Week* (September 13, 1982): 46.

640. "Imports Are down in Wake of War in South Atlantic; U.S. Embassy Outlines Appropriate Marketing Strategy." *Business America* 6 (May 2, 1983): 18–20.

641. Kelly, G. L. "Argentina: Array of Favorable Economic Factors Is Creating Another Billion-Dollar Market in Latin America." *Business America* 2 (May 21, 1979): 25–26.

642. Main, J. "The Argentinian Web Trapping U.S. Lenders." *Fortune* 110 (August 20, 1984): 122–26+.

643. "Outlook Is Encouraging for Economy and Inflation: Market Is Being Opened to Imports and Investment." *Business America* 3 (October 20, 1980): 38–39.

644. Siegelman, M. "Government Seeks Answers to Economy, Debt Problems." *Business America* 7 (August 20, 1984): 26–27.

645. Siegelman, M. "Modest Export Gains Seen, Would Be First since 1980." *Business America* 8 (March 4, 1985): 39–40.

646. Siegelman, M. "New Administration Seeks to Reactivate Economy." *Business America* 4 (July 27, 1981): 24–25.

647. Siegelman, M. "New Policies Are Aimed at Revitalizing Economy." *Business America* 5 (February 8, 1982): 18–19.

648. Siegelman, M. "Return to Democracy Boosts Confidence." *Business America* 7 (February 20, 1984): 31.

Colombia

649. "Growing Economy Requires U.S. Products and Services." *Business America* 3 (November 3, 1980): 24–25.

650. Muenzer, R. F. "Higher U.S. Sales Reflect Current Liberalization Policies." *Business America* 2 (July 30, 1979): 8.

651. Muenzer, R. F. "Real Growth to Increase as President Takes Helm." *Business America* 5 (August 9, 1982): 50–51.

652. Streitfeld, L. "Foreign Exchange Reserves, U.S. Market Share Mount." *Business America* 3 (July 28, 1980): 54.

Ecuador

653. "New Government Labels 1980 the Year of Production: Five-Year Economic Plan Outlines Fresh Opportunities." *Business America* 3 (March 24, 1980): 29–31.

Venezuela

654. "Easing of Financial Woes Yields Time to Focus on Renewing Economic Growth." *Business America* 8 (June 10, 1985): 23.

655. "Revival of Construction Could Stimulate U.S. Exports." *Business America* 3 (August 25, 1980): 23–24.

656. Siegelman, M. "Economic Upswing Predicted; U.S. Market Share Rises." *Business America* 4 (February 9, 1981): 52.

BANKING

Mexico

657. Daiboch, A. F. "U.S. Banks vs. the CCC [Commodity Credit]." *American Import/Export Management* 98 (February 1983): 10.

Latin America

658. "How Can American Banks Account for Those Latin Loans?" *Economist* 291 (June 2, 1984): 87–88.

659. Johnson, W. A. "Bank Size and U.S. Bank Lending to Latin America." *Federal Reserve Bank of New York Quarterly Review* 8 (Autumn 1983): 20–21.

660. "Latin America: Equity Vehicle for IDB" *Banker* 135 (April 1985): 11.

661. "Latin America: Growth in Energy Lending." *Petroleum Economist* 52 (June 1985): 219–20.

662. Poniachek, H. A. "U.S. International Banking and the Latin America Market." *Bankers Magazine* 166 (September/October 1983): 12–15.

Argentina

663. Bamber, Derek. "Argentina Survey [Economy and Banking]." *Euromoney* (January 1981): 37 page section following p. 80.

Chile

664. Letelier, L., and Moffitt, M. "How American Banks Keep the Chilean Junta Going." *Business & Society Review* (29) (Spring 1979): 42–51.

BALANCE OF PAYMENT

Mexico

665. Farrell, M. "International Impact of U.S. Money Supply: The Case of Mexico." *American Economic Review* 70 (June 1980): 433–43.

Latin America

666. Balassa, B. "Policy Responses to External Shocks in Selected Latin-American Countries." *Quarterly Review of Economics & Business* 21 (Summer 1981): 131–67.

667. Kemp, D. S., and Wilford, D. S. "Exchange Rates and the Balance of Payments in Latin America." *Business Economics* 14 (September 1979): 30–34.

668. Long, M. F. "External Debt and the Trade Imperative in Latin America." *Quarterly Review of Economics & Business* 21 (Summer 1981): 280–301.
669. Villares, P. "Latin America Must Export, Too [Nontraditional Products: To Reduce Deficits]." *Iron Age Metals Producer* 227 (July 2, 1984): 24.

Brazil

670. "The $6 Billion Scramble." *Economist* 286 (surv) (March 12, 1983): 11–12+.

BANK LOANS

Costa Rica

671. Holden, D. W. "Court to Costa Rica: Pay Up [Fidelity Union Loan]." *U.S. Banker* 96 (June 1985): 51.
672. Kallen, B. "Yes, We Have No Bananas [Fidelity Union: Demands Payment for Loan to Costa Rica]." *Forbes* 136 (July 1, 1985): 97.

Latin America

673. "$83 Million in Loans for Improving Transportation in Latin America and Caribbean Region." *Finance and Development* 18 (June 1981): 4–5.

MINERAL RESOURCES

Mexico

674. "DOE to Buy More Crude from Pemex for SPR." *Oil & Gas Journal* 79 (August 31, 1981): 114–15.
675. Ladman, Jerry R. "Mexican Petroleum and U.S. Mexican Trade." *Arizona Business* 28 (August/September 1981): 3–8.
676. "Mexico: A Face-Off with Exxon over High-Priced Oil." *Business Week* (August 10, 1981): 36.

677. "Mexico: Must You Take Our Water Too?" *Economist* 276 (July 5, 1980): 41–42.

678. Mumme, Steven P. "The Cananea Copper Controversy: Lessons for Environmental Diplomacy [Issue of Transboundary Air Pollution in the Planned Expansion of a Mexican Copper Smelter Company; Role of the International Banks; U.S. Economic Interests]." *Inter-American Economic Affairs* 38 (Summer 1984): 3–22.

679. Niering, F. E., Jr. "Mexico: Need to Regain Oil Exports." *Petroleum Economist* 52 (September 1985): 332–35.

680. United States. General Accounting Office. *Prospects for a Stronger United States-Mexico Energy Relationship; Report to the Congress by the Comptroller General of the United States.* Washington, DC: 1980. 64 p.

681. "U.S. Oil Imports: Mexico Remains Leading Supplier." *Petroleum Economist* 49 (December 1982): 484.

682. "U.S. Taps Mostly Mexican Crude for SPR Fill." *Oil & Gas Journal* 81 (December 5, 1983): 66.

683. "Why Won't the Mexicans Sell Us More Oil?" *Forbes* 124 (October 29, 1979): 41–52.

684. "Will the U.S. Find OPEC at Its Border?" *Business Week* (December 6, 1982): 49+.

Brazil

685. Cardoso, E. A. "The Burden of Exchange Rate Adjustment in Brazil." *Quarterly Review of Economics and Business* 21 (Summer 1981): 168–81.

686. "Gasohol Tax Break Gives Brazil a Bonanza." *Business Week* (June 23, 1980): 28.

Chile

687. "Chile: Boon for Mining Chemicals." *Chemical Week* 125 (December 12, 1979): 59–60.

688. "Sodium Nitrate Anti-Dumping Case Resolved; Olin Victory Means Large Duty for Chileans." *Chemical Marketing Reporter* 223 (March 21, 1983): 5+.

Colombia

689. Muenzer, R. F. "New Leaders Challenged; Hopes Pegged to Minerals." *Business America* 6 (February 21, 1983): 49–50.

690. "Some Southern Utilities Find It Cheaper to Import Coal." *Coal Age* 89 (May 1984): 19.

Venezuela

691. Jones, R. J. "Empirical Models of Political Risks in U.S. Oil Production Operations in Venezuela." *Journal of International Business Studies* 15 (Spring/Summer 1984): 81–95.

692. "New Development Plan May Help the Petroleum Industry Overcome Private-Sector Malaise and Spark Economy." *Business America* 5 (March 22, 1982): 24–26.

693. Sivesind, E. J. "Venezuela Oil." *Challenge* 23 (May/June 1980): 55–57.

694. "Synfuel Plant Is Bait for More Venezuelan Oil." *Chemical Week* 127 (October 15, 1980): 21.

695. "Venezuela Seeks Role in U.S. Energy Effort." *Oil and Gas Journal* 78 (March 31, 1980): 201.

696. "Venezuela to U.S.: Don't Impose Oil Import Fee." *Oil & Gas Journal* 83 (September 23, 1985): 66.

Reference Works

There are numerous sources on economic and business conditions in Latin America. The following sections identify government and private sources of information. From these basic sources of information, individuals can secure advice and assistance about conducting business activities in Latin America. Most of the reference material is in English, but a few of the major sources in Spanish have been listed.

GENERAL BIBLIOGRAPHIC REFERENCES

These publications are standard reference sources for Latin American business and economics.

697. *Business and Legal Aspects of Latin American Trade and Investment.* Center for Latin America, University of Wisconsin-Milwaukee, Milwaukee, WI 53201.
Contains current laws and regulations pertaining to trade and investment policies of Latin American countries.

698. *Copyright Protection in the Americas.* Oceana Publications, Inc., 75 Main St., Dobbs Ferry, NY 10522.
These volumes survey the copyright laws of the twenty-five Organization of American States (OAS) states. Annual supplements, Spanish and English.

699. *Corporate Taxation in Latin America.* International Bureau of Fiscal Documentation, Muiderpoort 124, Sorphatistraat, Amsterdam, The Netherlands.
Two volumes present complete range of tax laws, regulations, procedures, treaties, and taxation policies. Frequently updated.

700. *Digest of United States Practice in International Law.* U.S. Department of State, 2101 C St. N.W., Washington, DC 20520.
Provides information on development of international law. Annual publication.

701. *Economic and Social Progress in Latin America.* Inter-American Development Bank, Washington, DC 20057.
Analyzes regional economic and social developments. Detailed summaries for each country. Annual report.

702. *Economic Survey of Latin America.* U.N. Economic Commission for Latin America, 1801 K St., N.W., Washington, DC 20006.
Contains individual country reports. Summarizes Latin American economy annually. Statistical tables.

703. *Latin America.* Facts on File, Inc., 119 W. 57th St., New York, NY 10019.
Annual report of economic, political, diplomatic, and regional developments.

704. *Law of the Americas: An Introduction to the Legal Systems of the American Republics.* Oceana Publications, Inc., 75 Main St., Dobbs Ferry, NY 10522.
Chapters on laws in Latin America, inter-American laws, conventions, and treaties. Authors: Henry P. DeVries and José Rodríguez-Novás. Bibliography, 1965.

705. *Operating in Latin America's Integrating Markets: ANCOM/CACM/CARICOM/LAFTA.* Business International Corp., One Dag Hammarskjold Plaza, New York, NY 10017.
Discussion of the four regional economic units. Special emphasis on ANCOM, Decision 24, and its implications, 1977.

706. *Overseas Business Report: Marketing in* (Country). U.S. Department of Commerce, 14th St. and Constitution Ave., N.W., Washington, DC 20230.
An up-to-date source of current and detailed marketing information on each Latin American country. Annual report.

707. *Solving Latin American Business Problems.* Business International Corp., One Dag Hammarskjold Plaza, New York, NY 10017.
Case studies of problems faced by 200 U.S. firms operating in Latin American countries, 1968.

708. *Statement of the Laws of* (Country) *in Matters Affecting Business.* Organization of American States, Bureau of Legal Affairs, Washington, DC 20006.
Information for selected countries is provided on constitutions, current treaties, business regulations, taxation, and other policy items.

709. *Washington International Business Report.* International Business—Government Counsellors, Inc., 1625 Eye Street, N.W., Washington, DC 20006.
Up-to-date information on international trade and investment. Biweekly.

UNITED STATES GOVERNMENT PUBLICATIONS

A number of U.S. agencies publish material on business and economic subjects in Latin America. Of the agencies, the Departments of Commerce and State provide the best coverage. Publications usually have a modest fee. Information on materials published by these two agencies can be obtained from the following addresses:

Department of Commerce
14th St and Constitution Ave., N.W.
Washington, DC 20230

Department of State
2101 C St., N.W.
Washington, DC 20520

710. *Background Notes.* Department of State.
Memos on the political and economic structures of Latin American countries. Revised periodically.

711. *Business America* (formerly *Commerce America*). Department of Commerce. (Biweekly)
Up-to-date bulletin on business.

712. *Foreign Economic Trend Reports.* Department of Commerce.
Reports prepared by U.S. Foreign Service officials on individual countries.

713. *Global Market Survey.* Department of Commerce.
Reports on individual industries.

714. *International Marketing Newsmemos.* Department of Commerce.
Reports prepared by U.S. businessmen or Department of Commerce officials on countries, industries, and products.

715. *Key Officers of Foreign Service Posts: Guide for Business Representatives.* Department of State.
Lists names, addresses, telephone numbers of key foreign service officers.

716. *Overseas Business Reports.* Department of Commerce.
Marketing information on individual Latin American countries. Revised annually.

717. *Producer Goods Research.* Department of Commerce.
Information on foreign sales opportunities for American companies.

PERIODICALS

Periodicals provide current information on business and trade in Latin America.

718. *Boletin de Informacion Legal.* Instituto para la Integración de América Latina, Casilla de Correo 39, Sucursal 1, Buenos Aires, Argentina.
Surveys current economic legislation. Spanish.

719. *Business Latin America.* Business International Corp., One Dag Hammarskjold Plaza, New York, NY 10017.
Current economic news with a special section focusing on a single country.

720. *Latin American Economic Report.* William Holub, 432 Park Ave., S., New York, NY 10016. (Weekly)
Economic items on recent events.

721. *Novedades.* Inter-American Tax Research, Ltd., Pan Am Building, 200 Park Ave., New York, NY 10017. (Monthly)
Survey of taxation, industrial promotion laws, foreign investments, and trade for individual countries.

722. *Progreso: The Inter-American Economic and Business Review.* Vision, S.A., Carrera 14, No. 97-62, Bogota, Colombia. (9/yr.)
Covers Latin American business developments. Spanish.

723. *Quarterly Economic Review.* The Economist Intelligence Unit, Ltd., Spencer House, 27 St. James Place, London, England. (Quarterly)
Presents business outlook for the major Latin American countries.

724. *Review of the River Plate.* S.S. Koppe and Co., Inc., 19 W. 44th St., New York, NY 10036. (3/month)
Economic news of Argentina and other Latin American countries.

725. *The Times of the Americas.* The Times of the Americas, Woodward Building, Washington, DC 20005. (Biweekly)
Economic, political, and social happenings.

BANK PUBLICATIONS

The international banks of the United States and Europe publish excellent reports on business and economic conditions.

726. *Bank of London and South America Review.* Lloyds Bank International, Ltd., 40-66 Green Victoria St., London, England.
Covers a wide range of economic, political, and legal topics including banking, finance, trade, labor laws, foreign investment, and types of business enterprises.

727. *Investment Guides to Economic Reports on* (Country). Citibank, N.A., New York, NY 10043.
Investment information on individual countries. Published periodically.

728. *Report from the Bank of America's Man-on-the-Spot in* (Country). Bank of America, San Francisco, CA 94104.
Reports on business and finance from Latin American countries where Bank of America has representatives.

729. *World Guide for Exporters.* Chase Manhattan Bank, Chase World Information Corp., New York, NY 10015.
Annual report of export markets of countries. Updated monthly.

COMPANY PUBLICATIONS

A number of major accounting firms publish guides for doing business in Latin America. These guides present a wide range of information on business laws, operational procedures, business climate, international regulations, and like information. The countries covered in each of the publications vary, but all treat the major countries.

730. *Business Studies in* (Country). Touche Ross and Co., 1633 Broadway, New York, NY 10019.
731. *Characteristics of Business Entities:* (Country). Ernst and Ernst, International Operations, 153 E. 53d St., New York, NY 10022.
732. *Information Guide for Doing Business in* (Country). Price Waterhouse and Co., International Department, 1251 Avenue of the Americas, New York, NY 10020.
733. *Internal Tax and Trade Guide to* (Country). Peat, Marwick, Mitchell and Co., 345 Park Ave., New York, NY 10022.
734. *International Business Series:* (Country). Ernst and Ernst, International Operations, 153 E. 53d St., New York, NY 10022.
735. *International Tax and Business Service.* Deloitte, Haskins and Sells, 1114 Avenue of the Americas, New York, NY 10036.
736. *Tax and Trade Guide:* (Country). Arthur Andersen and Co., 69 W. Washington, Chicago, IL 60602.
737. *Tax Information Summaries:* (Country). Cooper and Lybrand, 1251 Avenue of the Americas, New York, NY 10020.

STATISTICAL HANDBOOKS

A number of statistical volumes are published providing basic data.

738. *America en Cifras.* Organization of American States, Washington, DC 20006.
739. *Boletin Estadistico.* Organization of American States, Washington, DC 20006.
740. *Statistical Abstract of Latin America.* Center of Latin American Studies, University of California-Los Angeles, Los Angeles, CA 90024.
741. *Statistical Yearbook for Latin America.* U.N. Economic Commision for Latin America, 1801 K St., N.W., Washington, DC 20006.

Appendices

Appendix A
United States Banks with
Latin American Relations

Within the United States, multinational banks and some regional banks have branches, affiliates, agencies, representative officers, or other facilities in Latin America. The major source of United States banks operating in Latin America is *Index to International Activities of United States Banks* published annually in March in a regular edition of the newspaper, the *American Banker*. This same edition contains a listing of foreign banks operating in the United States. A reprint of this information can be obtained from the American Bankers, 525 W. 42d St., New York, NY 10036.

INTERNATIONAL BANKS

Bank of America National Trust
   & Savings Association
Bank of America Center
555 California St.
San Francisco, CA 94104

Bank of London and South
   America
40166 Queen Victoria St.
London, England EC4P 4EL

Barclay's Bank of New York,
   N.A.
420 Lexington Ave.
New York, NY 10163

Chase Manhattan Bank, N.A.
1 Chase Manhattan Plaza
New York, NY 10081

Citibank, N.A.
399 Park Ave.
New York, NY 10022

First National Bank of Boston
100 Federal St.
Boston, MA 02110

Morgan Guaranty Trust
   Company of New York
23 Wall St.
New York, NY 10015

UNITED STATES REGIONAL BANKS

AmeriTrust Company
  900 Euclid Ave.
  Cleveland, OH 44101

Citizens and Southern National
  Bank
  35 Broad St., N.W.
  Atlanta, GA 30303

Continental Illinois National
  Bank and Trust Company of
  Chicago
  231 S. LaSalle St.
  Chicago, IL 60697

First Wisconsin National Bank of
  Milwaukee
  777 E. Wisconsin Ave.
  Milwaukee, WI 53202

Marine Midland Bank, N.A.
  One Marine Midland Center
  Buffalo, NY 14240

Mercantile Trust Company, N.A.
  8th & Locust Sts. & Mercantile
  Tower
  P.O. Box 524
  St. Louis, MO 63166

National Bank of Detroit
  Woodward Ave. at Fort St.
  Box 116
  Detroit, MI 48232

NCNB National Bank of North
  Carolina
  One NCNB Plaza
  Charlotte, NC 28255

Northwest Bank of Minneapolis,
  N.A.
  8th St. and Marquette Ave.
  Minneapolis, MN 55479

RepublicBank Dallas, N.A.
  P.O. Box 225961
  Pacific and Ervay Sts.
  Dallas, Texas 75265

Security Pacific National Bank
  Security Pacific Plaza
  333 S. Hope St.
  Los Angeles, CA 90071

Wells Fargo Bank, N.A.
  464 California St.
  San Francisco, CA 94163

Appendix B
Latin American Embassies in the United States

The Latin American embassies provide information and services to American industries and businesses. All embassies are located in Washington, DC.

Argentina Chancery
1600 New Hampshire Ave., N.W.
Washington, DC 20009
202-939-6400

Bahamas Chancery
600 New Hampshire Ave., N.W., Suite 865
Washington, DC 20037
202-338-3940

Barbados Chancery
2144 Wyoming Ave.
Washington, DC 20008
202-939-9200

Bolivia Chancery
3014 Massachusetts Ave., N.W.
Washington, DC 20008
202-483-4410

Brazil Chancery
3006 Massachusetts Ave., N.W.
Washington, DC 20008
202-797-0100

Chile Chancery
1732 Massachusetts Ave., N.W.
Washington, DC 20036
202-785-1746

Colombia Chancery
2118 Leroy Place, N.W.
Washington, DC 20008
202-387-8338

Costa Rica Chancery
2112 S St., N.W.
Washington, DC 20008
202-234-2945

Cuba (Cuban Office)
2630 16th St., N.W.
Washington, DC 20009
202-797-8518

Dominica Chancery
2025 I St., Suite 1125
Washington, DC 20006
202-467-5933

Dominican Republic Chancery
1715 22d St., N.W.
Washington, DC 20008
202-332-6280

Ecuador Chancery
2535 15th St., N.W.
Washington, DC 20009
202-234-7200

El Salvador Chancery
2308 California St., N.W.
Washington, DC 20008
202-265-3480

Grenada Chancery
1701 New Hampshire Ave.,
N.E.
Washington, DC 20009
202-265-2561

Guatemala Chancery
2220 R St., N.W.
Washington, DC 20008
202-745-4592

Guyana Chancery
2490 Tracy Place, N.W.
Washington, DC 20008
202-265-6900

Haiti Chancery
2311 Massachusetts Ave., N.W.
Washington, DC 20008
202-332-4090

Honduras Chancery
4301 Connecticut Ave., Suite
100
Washington, DC 20008
202-966-7700

Jamaica Chancery
1850 K St., N.W., Suite 355
Washington, DC 20006
202-452-0660

Mexico Chancery
2829 16th St., N.W.
Washington, DC 20009
202-234-6000

Nicaragua Chancery
1627 New Hampshire Ave.,
N.W.
Washington, DC 20009
202-387-4371

Panama Chancery
2862 McGill Terrace, N.W.
Washington, DC 20008
202-483-1407

Paraguay Chancery
2400 Massachusetts Ave., N.W.
Washington, DC 20008
202-483-6960

Peru Chancery
1700 Massachusetts Ave., N.W.
Washington, DC 20036
202-833-9860

Suriname Chancery
2600 Virginia Ave., N.W.,
Suite 711
Washington, DC 20037
202-338-6980

Trinidad and Tobago Chancery
1708 Massachusetts Ave., N.W.
Washington, DC 20036
202-467-6490

Uruguay Chancery
1918 F St., N.W.
Washington, DC 20006
202-331-1313

Venezuela Chancery
2445 Masachusetts Ave., N.W.
Washington, DC 20008
202-797-3800

Appendix C
United States Embassies or
Consulates in Latin America

The United States embassies are a major source of information for the businessman on the countries of Latin America. Within the embassies the key service positions for business and industrial information are the economic/commercial officer, financial attaché, political officer, consular officer, and public affairs officer. For each of the embassies the street address, telephone number, and the APO or FPO number is listed. To reach the embassy the APO or FPO number need only be used.

Argentina
    4300 Colombia, 1425
    Buenos Aires, Argentina
    Tel. 774-7611
    APO Miami 34034

Bahamas
    Mosmar Building
    Queen St.
    P.O. Box N-8197
    Nassau, Bahamas
    Tel. 809-322-1700

Barbados
    P.O. Box 302
    Bridgetown, Barbados
    Tel. 63574-7
    FPO Miami 34054

Belize
    Consulate General
    Gabourel Lane and Hutson St.
    Belize City, Belize
    Tel. (501) 7161

Bermuda
    Consulate General
    Vallis Building
    Front St.
    Hamilton, Bermuda
    Tel. 295-1342
    FPO NY 09560

Bolivia
    Banco Popular del Peru
        Building
    Corner of Calles Mercado and
        Colon
    P.O. Box 425
    La Paz, Bolivia
    Tel. 350251
    APO Miami 34032

Brazil
  Lote No. 3
  Avenida das Nocoes
  Brasilia, Brazil
  Tel. 061-223-0120
  APO Miami 34030

Chile
  Codina Building
  1343 Agustinas
  Santiago, Chile
  Tel. 710133/ 90
  APO Miami 34033

Colombia
  Calle 37, 8-40
  Bogota, Colombia
  Tel. 285-1300
  APO Miami 34038

Costa Rica
  Avenida 3 and Calle 1
  San Jose, Costa Rica
  Tel. 22-55-66
  APO Miami 34020

Cuba
  Swiss Embassy
  Calzada between L and M
  Vedado Section
  Havanna, Cuba
  Tel. 320551

Dominica
  Serviced by U.S. Embassy in
    Barbados

Dominican Republic
  Calle Cesar Nicolas Pensen and
    Calle Leopoldo Navarro
  Santo Domingo, Dominican
    Republic
  Tel. 682-2171
  APO Miami 34041

Ecuador
  Avenida 12 de Octubre y
    Avenida Patria
  Quito, Ecuador
  Tel. 548-000
  APO Miami 34039

El Salvador
  1230, 25 Avenida Norte
  San Salvador, El Salvador
  Tel. 26-7100
  APO Miami 34023-0001

Guatemala
  7-01 Avenida de la Reforma
  Zone 10
  Guatemala, Guatemala
  Tel. 31-15-41
  APO Miami 34024

Guyana
  31 Main St.
  Georgetown, Guyana
  Tel. 2-54901-9

Haiti
  Harry Truman Blvd.
  Port-au-Prince, Haiti
  Tel. 20354

Honduras
  Avenido La Paz
  Tegucigalpa, Honduras
  Tel. 32-3120
  APO Miami 34022

Jamaica
  Jamaica Mutual Life Center
  2 Oxford Rd., 3d Floor
  Kingston, Jamaica
  Tel. 809-92-94850

Mexico
  Paseo de la Reforma 305
  Mexico 5, D.F.
  Mexico, Mexico D.F.
  Tel. (525) 211-0042

Nicaragua
Km 4½ Carretera Sur
Managua, Nicaragua
Tel. 66010
APO Miami 34021

Panama
Avenida Balboa and Calle 38
Apartado 6959, R.P.5.
Panama, Panama
Tel. 27-1777
APO Miami 34002

Paraguay
1776 Avenida Mariscal Lopez
Asuncion, Paraguay
Tel. 201041/9
APO Miami 34036-0001

Peru
Avenida Inca Garcilaso de la
   Vega and Avenida Espana
Lima, Peru
Tel. 28600
APO Miami 34031

St. Lucia
Served by embassy in Barbados

Suriname
Dr. Sophie Redmondstraat 129
P.O. Box 1821
Paramaribo, Suriname
Tel. 72900

Trinidad and Tobago
15, Queen's Park West
P.O. Box 752
Port-of-Spain, Trinidad
Tel. 622-6271

Uruguay
Calle Lauro Müller 1776
Montevideo, Uruguay
Tel. 40-91-51
APO Miami 34035

Venezuela
Avenida Francisco de Miranda
   and Avenida Principal de la
   Floresto
Caracas, Venezuela
Tel. 284-7111
APO Miami 34037

Appendix D
Private Associations

A number of private associations provide information on doing business in Latin America.

American Bar Association. International Law Section, 1155 E. 50th St., Chicago, IL 60637.

The American Bar Association has a section on International Law. The section holds seminars, sponsors conferences, and prepares publications relating to Latin American trade and investments. The section has a standing committee on Inter-American Law.

American Management Association. Manager, International Division, American Management Association, 135 W. 50th St., New York, NY 10020.

Provides seminars on how to do business in specific Latin American countries. A publication program treating business negotiations, financing, exporting, industrial development, and other aspects is carried out. Films and cassettes of business negotiations are available.

Association of American Chambers of Commerce in Latin America. 1615 H St., N.W., Room 315, Washington, DC 20062.

This organization coordinates the activities of the American Chambers of Commerce in Latin America such as the Venezuelan-American Chamber of Commerce and Industry. These Latin Chambers of Commerce are excellent contacts for American businesses. Many are very helpful.

Council of the Americas. Director of Planning and Research Council of the Americas, 684 Park Ave., New York, NY 10021.

A private, nonprofit organization whose objective is to promote the role of private enterprise in the economic development of the Americas. Provides technical information and is active in bilateral business councils. Develops workshops and provides cassettes of them.

National Foreign Trade Council. 10 Rockefeller Plaza, New York, NY 10020.

This council collects and distributes information and materials concerning economic developments in the world. It publishes *Noticias, Weekly Digest of Hemispheric Reports*. There is an analysis of countries, industries and trends.

World Trade Institute. One World Trade Center, New York, NY 10048.

Provides a wide spectrum of information on world trade conditions. The World Trade Information Center has a computerized databank to provide information on names of manufacturers, importers and exporters of commodities for every country, tariff information, trade statistics, and government regulations.

Appendix E
Investment and Development Agencies

There are a number of investment and development agencies that are private or independently related to the U.S. government.

Export-Import Bank (Eximbank). Export-Import Bank of the United States, 811 Vermont Ave., N.W., Washington, DC 20571.
The Export-Import Bank is an independent agency of the U.S. government that works directly with private financial institutions to finance U.S. export sales. This is accomplished by loans and services. Seminars are conducted for business operations.

Foreign Credit Insurance Association. One World Trade Center, New York, NY 10048.
This is an association of stock and mutual insurance companies operating in partnership with the Export-Import Bank. A comprehensive selection of credit insurance policies are offered.

Overseas Private Investment Corporation. 1129 20th St., N.W., Washington, DC 20527.
This agency was created in 1969 by the Foreign Assistance Act to aid economic development in Third World countries. It does this by providing political risk insurance and financial assistance to support investments.

Private Export Funding Corporation. 280 Park Ave., New York, NY 10017.
This corporation is owned by fifty-four commercial banks, seven industrial corporations, and one investment banking firm. It makes loans to foreign, public, and private borrowers in order to purchase U.S. goods and services. Its loans are guaranteed by the Export-Import Bank.

Small Business Administration. 1441 L St., N.W., Washington, DC 20416.
This organization promotes international business through workshops, seminars, and conferences to inform businessmen of international marketing conditions. It offers financial assistance for developing and penetrating international markets.

Appendix F
Abbreviations of Agencies and Organizations

This glossary provides a convenient reference source for the identification of important abbreviations of agencies and organizations.

AAA—American Arbitration Association
AACCLA—Association of American Chambers of Commerce in Latin America
ABA—American Bar Association
AID—Agency for International Development
AMA—American Management Association
ANCOM—Andean Common Market
AP—Alliance for Progress
ASIL—American Society for International Law
BIC—Business International Corporation
CACM—Central American Common Market
CARICOM—Caribbean Community
CCPA—U.S. Court of Customs and Patent Appeals
CIA—U.S. Central Intelligence Agency
COA—Council of the Americas
DOC—Department of Commerce–U.S.
DOS—Department of State–U.S.
ECLA—United Nations Economic Commission for Latin America
Eximbank—Export-Import Bank
FCIA—Foreign Credit Insurance Association
FCPA—Foreign Corrupt Practices Act
GATT—General Agreement on Tariffs and Trade
GSP—Generalized System of Preferences
IABA—Inter-American Bar Association
IACAC—Inter-American Commercial Arbitration Comission
IACCP—Inter-American Council for Commerce and Production
IACIC—Inter-American Convention on International Commercial Arbitration
IBRD—International Bank for Reconstruction and Develoment (World Bank)

ICC—International Chamber of Commerce
ICCA—International Council for Commercial Arbitration
ICSID—International Center for the Settlement of Investment
    Disputes
IDB—Inter-American Development Bank
IFC—International Finance Corporation
ILO—International Labor Organization
IMF—International Monetary Fund
ITC—International Trade Commission
LAFTA—Latin American Free Trade Association
LC—Library of Congress
MIFT—Mexican Institute for Foreign Trade
MTN—Multilateral Trade Negotiations
NFTC—National Foreign Trade Council
OAS—Organization of American States
OECD—Organization for Economic Corporation and Development
OPIC—Overseas Private Investment Corporation
PEFCO—Private Export Funding Corporation
SBA—Small Business Administration
SEC—Securities and Exchange Commission
UNCITRAL—United Nations Commission on International Trade
    Law
UNCTAD—United Nations Conference on Trade and Development
WTI—World Trade Institute

Author Index

Numbers refer to citation numbers, not page numbers.

Title Index

Numbers refer to citation numbers, not page numbers.

Subject Index

Numbers in italics refer to page numbers. All other numbers refer to citation numbers.